LEAKING

Addressing Addiction Counselor Codependency

D1210991

Mary Crocker Cook, D.Min, LMFT, LAADC, CADCII

Author of *Awakening Hope* and *Afraid to Let Go*

Leaking. Addressing Addiction Counselor Codependency

ISBN: 978-1-61170-225-5

Published in the USA by:

 Robertson Publishing™
www.RobertsonPublishing.com

Printed in the USA, UK, and Australia on acid-free paper.

To purchase additional copies of this book go to:
amazon.com
barnesandnoble.com

Other titles by Mary Cook:

Awakening Hope. A Developmental, Behavioral, Biological Approach to Codependency

Afraid to Let Go. For Parents of Adult Addicts and Alcoholics

Codependency and Men. Where Early Attachment, Gender Role, and Adrenal Fatigue Meet

Wake Them Up. They'll Listen to You. Psychoeducation Strategies for Chemical Dependency Counselors. Co-author, Chris Packham.

Welcome to My World. (A novel) A week in the life of a substance abuse counselor.

The Work Goes On. (A Novel) Another week in the live of a substance abuse counselor.

Don't Leave!!! Codependency and Attachment

Into Solution. Daily Support for Recovery Treatment Center Staff

Dedication

To my colleagues in recovery.
We need to put the oxygen mask on first!

Table of Contents

Why Do We Need This Book?

I have spent more than 25 years training chemical dependency counselors, they are my favorite people. For the most part, they're either in personal addiction recovery or they are family members who have been touched by the chaos of addiction. The very passion that brings us to this work is the potential foundation for burnout and relapse if those issues are not identified and addressed throughout a counselor's career.

I plan to address codependency from early attachment disruption perspective, which results in both codependent behaviors as well as immune system damage. When I see counselors relapse or abruptly leave a career they trained to enter I always wonder about the triggers they faced that they couldn't manage without imploding. Our clients and co-workers can put their finger on our unhealed wounds on a regular basis due to our ability to identify with them. In fact, our identification is a mixed blessing. We can draw compassion from our ability to identify. We can also step into blind spots and reactivity that may go unchecked without proper support and awareness.

Working with a population that is cognitively impaired, emotionally reactive and defensive, has difficulty attaching in healthy ways, with profound trust issues is a challenge that only people with a calling will enter and remain. It is not a sponsorship with a check situation — it's a job. The majority of our co-workers may very well have some of those same clients' traits, even with years of sobriety. We earn every dollar we get and we don't get enough of those.

I have been at this job for less than 1 year and 5 people have died. The reasons for death have ranged from heart attack, being beaten, being hit by a car while on a bike, and two unknown causes, but most likely as a result of something to do with drugs — an overdose, a medical condition that developed because of drug use, or some sort of violence that may have occurred during the drug sale transaction. In addition to the mentioned deaths, there is more disease, sickness, and injury behind the walls of the clinic per person than there is in public places. People have heart conditions, hypertension, diabetes, walk with a cane or need assistance to walk, infections, hepatitis C, muscular sclerosis, sleep apnea, a multitude of dental problems, including missing teeth, and much more...

CD Counselor in a Residential Treatment Program

Despite the challenges, there are the rewards. There are the clients that call us on their fifth sobriety birthday to thank us. There are the families that reunite and heal together. There are the children reunited with their parents. And there are the communities that regain hope for the future.

I ran into an old client at the movie theater. It took me a few minutes to recognize him because he looked physically different. When I worked with him, he was newly clean from abusing cocaine. Fast forward 1 year, he is clean, newly promoted at his job, and engaged. He looked so happy and so healthy. It was a shock to me because when he left our program, while he technically graduated, he was receiving multiple probation violations and his probation officer would tell us he was at risk for being re-arrested. To see him again was a shock because last news I heard, he was 1 step away from re-incarceration. These small glimpses really help me through the hard days; we experience so much loss in this field but success is there too.

CD Counselor in IOP Program

One client at a time we take on a fearsome enemy — the disease of addiction. Alcoholics Anonymous is right when it describes addiction as "cunning, baffling and powerful," and we are required to stand still and also wade into some dark, trauma-based situations sometimes. And we do it over and over again. Without self-care, we will erode like a rock pounded by water, and even the best-intentioned counselors will begin to lose heart for their work. We run out of energy and hope and begin to feel like Sisyphus, pushing the rock up the hill over and over again. We can become demoralized and even cynical which carries over to our co-workers, and even clients. In fact, in my experience co-workers can be harder than the clients because the triggering client will eventually leave the facility. I may be working side-by-side with my challenging colleague for years.

This past week I had a client that had been doing very well for about 6 months. He caved to his anger that lead to a residential discharge and a subsequent relapse. This is a chronic alcohol abuser with multiple medical issues due to his history of substance use. He came into the office under the influence with a great deal of suicidal and homicidal ideation. He referenced another client who had recently passed, assumed to be from his own substance abuse. After trying to put the client on a hold, he ended up getting arrested for a violation of his parole. After it was all done, I wanted to cry. However, due to time constraints and paperwork that has to be done, there was no time. I found that I was snappy with my colleagues. I don't like being like that. I knew that I was upset because the client was referencing another client who had passed and I knew the reality for this client, based on his history and medical issues, would likely be a premature outcome for him too. I was having a strong reaction to the situation for many reasons. I like this client; I liked this other client who passed and hoped the best for both of them; and all of it within a short period of time.

CD Counselor in a Co-occurring Treatment Program

This book is written to preserve and address the counselors in the field. The front line counselors who choose to get up and do this work day after day draw on their internal and spiritual strength to have and communicate hope when it sometimes seems doubtful. You are my heroes.

CHAPTER ONE

The Set-Up

The definition of codependency:

At its heart, codependency is a set of behaviors developed to manage the anxiety that comes when our primary attachments are formed with people who are inconsistent or unavailable in their response to us. Our anxiety-based responses to life can include over-reactivity, image management, unrealistic beliefs about our limits, and attempts to control the reality of others. This occurs to the point where we lose our boundaries, self-esteem and even our own reality. Ultimately, codependency is a chronic stress disease which can devastate our immune system and lead to systemic, even life-threatening illness.

Awaking Hope. A Developmental, Behavioral, Biological Approach to Codepedency Treatment.
Mary Crocker Cook

There's something about the backgrounds of chemical dependency counselors that draws them to the counseling profession. There are 23 million recovering people in the United States, and they do not all choose to enter the treatment field. Some people enroll in addiction studies training convinced that their life experience is the only tool they have to make a living because they have no other legal employment background. Drawing from a sponsorship model is not a sustaining motivation, and over the years I have observed that these counselors frequently don't complete their studies, or they don't pursue the counseling work over time. Becoming a counselor represents a lot of academic work, and it requires us to collect more than 4,000 hours. This level of commitment, without a large paycheck, can be discouraging. For example, I might have 100 people start a semester and will graduate 25 students two years later. It is the 25 who complete the two years, and then the 20 of them who take their certification exam who are in it for the long haul. Who are these 20 people?

They have been affected by the disease of addiction and have survived.

There is a level of patience and tolerance required to work with addicts and alcoholics going through early recovery that the average person doesn't possess. When people are loaded they demonstrate BAD behavior like lying, conning, cheating, manipulating, scamming, intimidation and stealing. They throw up on themselves, pee on the couch, forget to shower, smell like chemicals, slur their speech, have nasty mood swings, disappear for days and can be unpredictable. These are not necessarily permanent character traits. We also know that when people get clean and cognitively clear, they can make better decisions and cooperate in their recovery. We know because we entered recovery and we've seen so many others do the same thing.

We can also tolerate the chaos because we learned to manage emotional unavailability and emotional volatility early in our lives. We learned coping skills at the knees of the adults in our lives who may have been under the influence, clinically depressed, criminally active, unfaithful, physically and emotionally absent, or physically and sexually abusive. We are RESILIENT. However, our coping and resilience came at a price, a price our bodies may still be paying years later. It's a price that makes us vulnerable to chronic illness without intervention and support.

Foundation for Secure Attachment

For healthy trust to develop between a child and a caretaker, and later for counselor and client, there needs to be consistent and responsive bonding and attachment.

Bonding refers to the parents' emotional investment in their child, which builds and grows with repeated meaningful shared experiences. Bonding only happens through shared time and experience.

Attachment usually refers to the tie between the infant and parents, which the child actively initiates and participates in. Attachment needs mean that the child will try to engage the caretaker to notice their attempts and respond positively and consistently so the child feels seen and heard.

The quality of attachment largely impacts the child's developing sense of self and approach to the world environment.

Secure attachments develop as a result of consistent and accurate response between the caregiver and child. Accurate responses require the caregiver to be emotionally, cognitively and physically present in a predictable and meaningful way to participate in the developing relationship over time.

Even as adults we experience threats and anxiety, and our instinct is to reach out to someone we trust. When we experience **Secure attachment** as an adult, it will look like this:

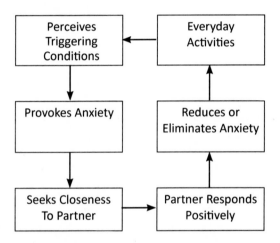

Jim has just completed an intake with a resistant client who clearly resents being in an addiction treatment center. The client attempts to intimidate Jim with aggressive body language and verbal hostility. Jim uses every bit of energy he has to stay level and calm, but he hears himself getting a little louder in response. Jim even uses sarcasm towards the client at the end of the intake. Jim barely communicates to his co-workers the rest of the day. He is clearly angry and shut down and unwilling to talk about it with them other than to call the new client a "knucklehead." On his drive home, he tailgates and flips off another driver, yelling "asswipe" as he drives off.

When he gets home he can feel that his shoulders are tight; he's irritable, and he just wants to hide in the garage. Jim's wife, Carol, notices his body language when he arrives and feels a little stung at first by his one-word answers and by his refusal to help her in the kitchen. While she angrily thinks to herself, "WTF?" and immediately wants to follow him outside, she takes a breath and remembers that everything was fine between them that morning. Instead of taking it personally she goes into the garage with a small snack and asks Jim about his day. At first Jim is still grumpy, but as Carol shares a little about her day, Jim decides to open up to her and tells her about being triggered by the hostile client. The client tried to bully him the way his dad bullied him as a kid. He admits that he wanted to punch the guy in the face, which makes him a little ashamed of himself — "I thought I was better than that." Carol can be compassionate without problem-solving. After a few minutes, Jim accepts her hug and follows her back into the kitchen to finish up dinner and watch a favorite TV show together.

When we're securely attached to someone we can trust we can be real with them, and conflict will not be a deal breaker. They can see us with our flaws or struggles, and they will hang in there because the relationship matters to them. WE matter to them. Some of us will experience this for the first time with a sponsor or maybe a trusted therapist.

When we don't have this secure foundation, we become anxiously attached codependents. We don't trust the attachment of others to us and fear that they will abandon us. Or we may be avoidantly attached codependents and don't allow ourselves to attach and depend on those who might abandon us.

Relationship Disruption

Attachments can get interrupted in childhood for a variety of reasons:

- Extended periods of illness (parent or child)
- Hospitalization due to physical or mental illness
- Placement in the foster care system
- Serious mental illness creating emotional and mental unavailability
- Abusive relationships that absorb the majority of the caretaker's energy
- Incarceration

- Alcohol/Drug addiction
- Military deployment

None of these reasons have anything to do with LOVE for the child.

However, the child cannot possibly know this and they end up believing that the unavailable parent is not available due to some defect within the child. We believe that if we were "enough" the parent would CHOOSE to be available. This begins the "going to the hardware store to get milk" pattern we talk about in Al-Anon. We approach unavailable people as though they are withholding from us rather than accepting that they are not emotionally available. The trick is to approach emotionally available people.

Anxious Attachment

When our caregiver is unpredictably available, and her emotional response is unreliable, we stay watchful for signs that she will see and hear us. Our energy goes into learning "her" patterns and meeting her needs in order to get our own needs addressed. The parent's responses are internally consistent but unfortunately, are unpredictable to anyone else, including the child. ***The child feels powerless to control or predict his/her experience*** because the response will be unpredictably supportive or hostile. That response may create learned helplessness and limit risk-taking and exploration.

Our confidence in ourselves to respond appropriately to relationship and personal threats with self-soothing strategies doesn't develop adequately because all of our coping mechanisms are being developed to manage external threats to our security. We don't learn how to manage our emotions; we can't regulate our own anxiety, so we are looking outside of ourselves to find a solution. That solution might be chemicals, porn or another person.

If we are ***anxiously attached*** and get triggered as an adult, it might look like this:

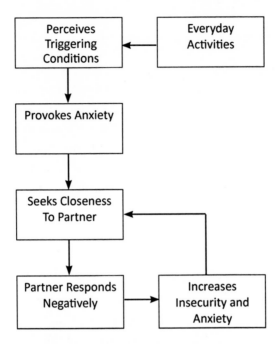

Melissa notices that her co-worker on the treatment unit, John, seems to be preoccupied, and barely responds when Melissa tries to chat with him in the morning. Melissa can feel her stomach knot up, but decides to try not to think about it as she goes into group. Group is a great distraction, but when she gets back to the office she shares with John, she finds herself watching him closely for signs that he's mad at her. Her mind starts racing through all the possible reasons he isn't talking to her: "What did I say?" "What did I do?". Melissa finds it hard to focus on writing up her group progress notes. Melissa thinks of a question she can ask John to find out how he's feeling about her, instead of asking him directly due to fear of his answer. Instead, she pays close attention to his tone of voice when he answers, again looking for clues about his feelings about her. The more she focuses on figuring out what John's "deal" is and if it's about her, the less she focuses on what she needs to do.

Once an anxiously attached codependent is hijacked by their fear of a "problem" in a relationship that may result in the relationship ending, they cannot shift this thought. It's what they think about, talk about, worry about. They find it almost impossible to reassure themselves or calm themselves down.

Andrew is running late for staff meeting due to an emergency dental appointment this morning. As he slides into his seat in staffing, he catches the clinical director looking quickly away from him. Later on, he realizes that the clinical director has not said anything to him during the meeting. The longer the meeting goes, the more anxious Andrew becomes. He finds himself doodling on his notepaper trying to manage the feeling that he's going to come out of his skin. As a result, when the clinical director finally does address him, he doesn't hear him and the clinical director has to call his name to get his attention. At this point Andrew is mortified, sure that he is seen as a "dumb-ass" and begins to worry about his job.

Both Andrew and Melissa do not trust that they can simply ask the other person what might be going on with them. Being direct may "open a can of worms," and they're afraid of the criticism and blame that is sure to follow the question. What if their question pisses the other person off so much that the relationship is damaged? Ironically, by acting out instead of simply asking the question, they are more likely to create a problem because they are acting oddly or insecurely.

Avoidant Attachment

Rather than unpredictable responses from caregivers, some children do not receive a response when they try to attach. The avoidant child learns that seeking closeness through crying and clinging is futile. They learn that it more likely results in parental withdrawal or even punishment. The very person who is supposed to provide the reassurance becomes the source of pain. Instead, independence is reinforced and valued. As a result, attempts to attachment decrease and detachment behaviors become prominent.

If we are triggered as adults, the ***avoidant codependent*** might look like this:

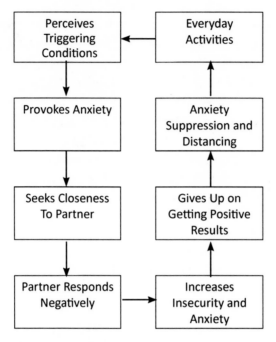

Jose is the oldest of a large immigrant family who carried a great deal of responsibility for his younger brothers and sisters. He was expected to be a role model and was working and going to school as soon as he was old enough to be hired. Jose's father worked two jobs to support his large growing family. His mother cleaned houses to help make ends meet. The only time Jose would spend with his father was on Saturday night when the men in the family would come over, drink beer and listen to music. Jose's parents were frequently exhausted. By the time they put everyone to bed, there was no energy or time left over if Jose would try to ask them for advice or support. Jose received a lot of praise for his independence, his responsibility, and his ability to make money and take care of himself. Jose learned early on that to be a "man" meant to handle his own business unless he was drunk and could be irresponsible.

With three years of sobriety, Jose is already a team lead on his treatment unit. He is first to arrive and last to leave. Without alcohol, Jose is NEVER less than responsible, and he is quick to judge others who don't match his work ethic. Early one morning, Jose received a text that his daughter needed him to pick her up after school, which conflicted with a group he was going to lead. Jose mentioned that he "might need some coverage later in the day" to his team as he passed them in the hall. When no one volunteered, Jose texted his daughter that she has to call her mother and then he carried an attitude the rest of the day. It never occurred to Jose that his team wasn't clear because he didn't ask for something specific — they didn't know when he needed help or with what. As far as Jose is concerned it's a reminder that, "as usual" people don't have his back.

Avoidant codependents can be hard to get to know. While they are super responsible, they are unwilling to depend on others to meet their needs and wants. This lack of trust makes codependents hard to give to or work with as a colleague. They don't work well as a team unless they can be the leader because they are the only person they trust. Sadly, their willingness to walk away from relationships gives others the impression that they don't care. In fact, they care SO MUCH that they are terrified of allowing themselves to need or want other people in fear of being betrayed or disappointed. It is easier to limit their investment then face the pain they believe is inevitable when the relationship ends.

Taneasha was the only child of a single mom whose father left the family when Taneasha was two years old. Her mom was not well educated and scrambled to make ends meet. Her mom decided to go back to school and get a law degree at night, which took a long time due to her part-time schedule. As a result, Taneasha learned to cook and get her homework done with very little supervision. Taneasha watched her mom battle with depression on top of her intense schedule. When her mother did have down time away from her studies, she would hide in her room and watch T.V., and react with irritability and impatience if Tanaesha tried to come into her room for company. It was clear that Taneasha was a "burden" when her mother was down.

Taneasha has been working on the co-occurring disorders unit for the last year, and her employers had not followed through with the training they had promised her when she took the job. She is spending her nights and weekends trying to figure out the "mental health" thing. She figures that if they were too busy to train her, they would be really irritated if she acted "needy" asking for help. Instead, Taneasha just struggles through and doesn't tell anyone. "I'll figure it out," she tells herself.

It doesn't occur to either Jose or Taneasha to ever ask for help or ask for feedback. They take pride in their independence and resiliency, and in some ways, they should. They've raised themselves pretty well. On the other hand, working cooperatively or allowing themselves to be vulnerable feels impossible for them. It's incredibly hard for them to have a satisfying relationship. They are the only ones they truly trust.

Attachment and Psychological Openness

Attachment styles affect the way we engage with the outside world, as well as how we respond to feedback and new information. In many ways, attachment style connects with our ability to be teachable. Secure attachment is correlated with cognitive openness — the ability to tolerate ambiguity and the freedom to integrate new information and perspectives. Because **securely attached** people are not anticipating relationship disruption, they are not looking for a threat in new information or feedback. While the feedback can be disappointing or even hurt their feelings, they don't draw the conclusion that the relationship is about to end as a result. In fact, they trust that the relationship will be what helps them work through the process.

Kaylie is surprised when she comes across a printed email exchange between her clinical supervisor and her co-worker amongst the papers stacked near the copy machine. While she has been filling out financial aid paperwork for her son, anxious about how she will pay for his education, the email seems to hint at a large raise offered to her coworker who carries the same caseload that she carries. Kaylie feels her heart stop for a moment, and then takes a breath and decides to ask her supervisor about it after the staff meeting that afternoon. Kaylie takes a few minutes that afternoon to call her sponsor and talk through her fears, realizing that she receives great feedback from her clients and coworkers, and it is possible that there is more to learn. She decides not to get upset until she has all the information.

On the other hand, **anxiously attached** people are often preoccupied by the threatening aspects of new information. They are quick to worry about the hidden meanings and underlying messages behind the information, and worry about possible changes to a relationship as a result of new information. These worries prompt secretiveness and withholding of information due to worry about what others may think or say in response. It also prompts an unwillingness to ask questions or ask for information directly. The possibility of causing a conflict or "bad" reaction leads to passivity or even denial. Supervising an anxious staff member can be irritating because they are not straightforward — you have to pull the information out of them.

Over dinner, Jason's wife, Carolyn, tells him that she has been struggling with her energy levels lately and finding it hard to get out of bed in the morning. She has seen her primary doctor who has referred her to a therapist to be evaluated for depression. Jason can feel his heart start to race. Everyone he knows that has been to counseling got a divorce, and he begins to challenge the doctor's recommendation. He begins to accuse Carolyn of poor diet and exercise regimens, which would probably clear the whole thing up if she applies herself. Carolyn leaves the table in tears, validating Jason's worst fear that this is the beginning of the end. Jason is distracted and a mess at work the next day, and blames his case load when his supervisor questions him.

Avoidantly attached people overemphasize self-reliance, and so habitually reject any new information that might demand a revision of their beliefs. They are quick to say, "I already knew that," or reject the information outright, filled with defensive arguments and justifications. Giving them feedback is very difficult because they interpret their lack of knowledge as a failure or weakness in some way. They MUST be all knowing when they are completely self-reliant. Supervising an avoidant staff member is exhausting and being honest with prickly co-workers feels like a chore.

Benjamin is dreading the upcoming review with his primary counselor, Lou. Every year Benjamin always feels like he has wrestled an alligator trying to give Lou feedback. No matter how neutral he tries to be, Lou responds with lists of defensive explanations and excuses for every suggestion Benjamin makes. Lou feels like Benjamin has been keeping a list of his "failures" to use against him in their yearly conversation, so Lou feels he HAS to defend himself in order keep his job. Benjamin has not idea that Lou feels like his job is on the line – thought it does cross Benjamin's mind during the review!

People who are resilient tend to be cognitively flexible – flexible in the way they think about challenges and flexible in the way they react emotionally to stress. They are not wedded to a specific style of coping. Instead they shift from one coping strategy to another depending on the circumstances. Many are able to accept what they cannot change; to learn from failure; to use emotions like grief and anger to fuel compassion and courage; and to search for meaning in adversity.

Acceptance

Accepting the reality of our situation, even if that situation is frightening or painful, is an important component of cognitive flexibility. To remain effectively engaged in problem-oriented and goal-directed coping we must keep our eyes wide open and acknowledge, rather than ignore, potential roadblocks. Avoidance and denial are generally counterproductive mechanisms that may help us cope for a while, but ultimately they stand in the way of growth, interfering with the ability to actively solve problems.

Sometimes acceptance involves not only acknowledging the reality of one's situation, but also accepting what can and cannot be changed, abandoning goals that no longer seem feasible, and intentionally re-directing efforts toward that which can be changed. So, acceptance is not the same as resignation and does not involve giving up or quitting. It is grounded in "realistic optimism."

In their book, The Resilience Factor, Karen Reivich and Andrew Shatte refer to "realistic optimism." Like pessimists, realistic optimists pay close attention to negative information that is relevant to the problems they face, however, unlike pessimists, they do not remain focused on the negative. They tend to disengage rapidly from problems that appear to be unsolvable. That is they know when to cut their losses and turn their attention to problems that they believe they can solve.

Frank has been suffering from frequent migraines. Sometimes they are so bad he starts to vomit and has to leave the treatment program and go home. Frank's colleague, Sandy, is worried about him and decides to drop by his apartment after work to check on him and bring some soup. As Frank opens the door he looks terrible, and he sees the worry in Sandy's eyes. Grateful for the soup, they sit down at the table, and

Frank begins to confide his growing struggle to go to work since the new clinical director came on board. Frank honestly feels he should have been promoted to the position, despite the fact that he did not have as much education or experience as the new director. For Frank it was a loyalty issue. As Frank and Sandy talk Frank realizes how personally he has taken what was essentially a business decision, and Sandy proposes that Frank consider finishing his education to make him a more viable candidate in the future. Maybe this is the "wake-up" call Frank needs to do what he already knew he needed to do but was putting off!

Cognitive flexibility may lead to cognitive reframing of painful situations allowing us to find meaning, gratitude, humor and purpose in the situation we have been fighting or regretting. Humor is especially associated with areas of the brain that are involved in cognitive appraisal as well as reward and motivation, capacities that appear to be associated with resilience.

What Secure Interactions Are Supposed To Look Like

Secure interactions require basic abilities to self-regulate. Heller and Lapierre define this as, *"When we are tired, we can sleep, and when we are stressed we have healthy ways to relieve that stress. Affect regulation involves how we manage our emotions. Symptoms of emotional dysregulation develop when we are unable to feel our emotions, when they overwhelm us or when they remain unresolved."*

Effective communication in a trusting relationship requires the presence and ability to both ask for a response and to respond promptly.

Asking for a Response

Clearly signaling the need for support: *"I really could use some help with this client. I can't seem to get through to him. What might I be missing?"*

Maintaining signals until they are detected: *"I can see this might not be a good time to talk about next week's schedule. I'll remind you at the meeting tomorrow, okay?"*

Openness to the partner's response: *"I can hear that you are really frustrated with me. I DID say I would take your group tomorrow, and I double booked. Let's figure it out."*

Finding comfort in an appropriate response: *"I appreciate that you're willing to own your part of the screw-up yesterday. I feel better."*

Responding Appropriately

Detecting the partner's implied or implicit requests for secure base support: *"You've been sitting there pretty quietly for the last hour. Do you need to talk to me about something?"*

Correctly interpreting the request: *"So, you want me to set up some time for us to talk later today?"*

Responding appropriately and promptly: *"I hear that you're really worried. It sounds like we need to make time to talk about this as soon as we can."*

Chapter Two

Codependent Counselor Behaviors

Can you be both anxious and avoidant? You bet. The key is that your working model of a relationship is that both people are not emotionally available AT THE SAME TIME. So, I can be the anxious, intrusive, freaked out one or the detached, observing, quick to run away avoidant one. What they have in common is:

I Don't Trust The Relationship is Solid

Peter has been working in addiction treatment for ten years and has developed a strong reputation in the field. He was recently promoted to a clinical supervisor position when his supervisor took a job with another agency, and Peter was the logical choice. Suddenly he was no longer a coworker but the manager. He was unprepared for the shift in power. Peter's wife is worried because he no longer seems off-duty. They have dinner, family events, even attempts to get away that are interrupted by crisis phone calls from the staff. Peter sees this level of availability as required, feeling responsible for meeting the needs of his staff because he can relate to their struggles even though he's technically their boss. He wants to stay part of the team and feels sick inside when he sees the increasing gap between his staff and himself. Peter has even occasionally cried when alone after staff meetings and has increased his blood pressure medicine. He feels like he's losing it and wonders if he needs to see a psychiatrist and get on some meds.

Let's take a look at the codependent symptoms that develop as a result of anxious and avoidant attachment, and how they play out in the treatment arena. Keep in mind that we develop behavioral strategies to make the disrupted attachments in our early lives manageable. Our behavioral responses to manage our unavailable caregivers makes sense in context – think of them as outdated strategies for survival.

Symptom One: Lack of Attunement with Self

Avoiding awareness of our reality is often an attempt to deny thoughts, desires or intentions that we feel will threaten or contradict the needs of those with whom we feel a strong attachment. We instinctively hide feelings and thoughts we assume to be threatening to other people (and might cause them to leave us). We have lost touch with what we need, feel and think. We disappear and can be invisible to ourselves. Our reactions to events and people can catch us off guard because we are not paying attention to ourselves. We don't realize we are tired, stressed, that our back hurts or that our feelings have been hurt. So when we act out, we are just as surprised as everyone else.

Tom has been working in the addicted offender re-entry program for the last five years. He has tremendous empathy for the guys due to his own history of incarceration and has an amazing amount of patience, even when the other counselors are tearing their hair out. One afternoon Tom's co-worker heard raised voices in Tom's office and called their supervisor to check on Tom. When they opened the door, Tom was red in the face and not making much sense as he screamed at the client in front of him. Tom abruptly stopped when he saw them and began to hyperventilate. Unable to catch his breath, Tom's supervisor had Tom sit down, and grabbed a lunch bag for him to breathe into. After a few minutes, Tom was able to talk again and had no idea what had happened. It was as though he had "blacked out."

As his supervisor later processed the incident with Tom they realized Tom hadn't taken a lunch and had an apple for breakfast almost eight hours ago. He had slept poorly the last two nights because he has a cold he isn't treating. He also had not been setting boundaries with the client he was yelling at who had already turned in two dirty tests. Tom was referred to the EAP by his supervisor who also insisted that Tom stay home for a couple of days to rest and take care of himself. When Tom thought more about it, he realized he hadn't been to a meeting in almost a month and had not been calling his sponsor.

This situation is all too common in chemical dependency treatment. We are usually short staffed and lack enough resources. People will not carve out time for lunch or exercise, or even their own recovery program. They tell themselves, "I'm doing recovery all day," when the reality is they are helping other people work THEIR program; the counselor is not attending to their own recovery needs. When we lack an internal observer we cannot recognize ourselves physically, emotionally, intellectually or spiritually. It is as though we have to walk around the world asking others, "Do I look like her?" "Do I sound like him?" When we lack an internal observer we cannot self-correct and identify our blind spots. We are unable to establish effective boundaries and instead are vulnerable to subtle and constant merging with those around us.

Our lack of boundaries can be painfully obvious to everyone but ourselves because we are so disconnected with our actual agendas, needs and wants.

With **internal boundaries**, I can retain my feelings and thoughts even when yours are different and find this curious or interesting rather than threatening. I can see your behavior and feelings as "information" rather than cues to my next "move" in the interaction and not feel "responsible" for your thoughts and behavior. With internal boundaries I am aware that you have an entire internal life that has NOTHING to do with me and does not require my intervention or advice or assistance.

With Internal Boundaries

I am in control of how much information I share about me, based on our level of intimacy and trust.

I recognize that trust takes time, I cannot have "instant intimacy" and still be selective and self-protective.

I will share with safe people and withhold from unsafe people, and internal boundaries allow me see who is who!

With External Boundaries

I am in control of my physical self.

I have control over the space around me I am in control of my possessions.

I have choices about how close I get to you physically and sexually.

I can choose based on my comfort zone, our level of intimacy, how much time I am willing to spend with you.

I decide whether or not I want to participate in shared activities.

Boundaries and a separate sense of "self" allow me to use my judgment to take calculated risks about how much I want to invest in relationships and activities. Boundaries will tell me when someone is pushing me somewhere I do not want to go.

Boundaries allow me to disengage rather than to keep on trying to make dysfunctional situations "work." I have internal permission to make decisions based on my welfare and not just what is "best" or most comfortable for the people around me.

Symptom Two: Lack of Attunement with Others

Frequently codependents have not developed an understanding of other people's thoughts and emotions, and can lack empathy. We have difficulty with inferring and predicting another person's plans, intentions, and motives, despite the fact that we are always monitoring them to figure out how we should act.

Modern emotion theories take as their foundation theory developed by Silvan Tompkins. Tompkins argued that affect, or emotion, results from the brain's responses to stimulant that, in turn, sets off various reposes in the body that compel us to pay attention. According to Tomkins, a central characteristic of affect is affective resonance, which refers to a person's tendency to resonate and experience the same affect in response to viewing a display of that affect by another person, sometimes thought to be "contagion." Affective resonance is considered to be the original basis for all human communication (before there were words, there was a smile and a nod). Affect, or emotions, is the link between need, recognizing the need, and later relief that allows us to use or emotions as an important source of information. Mirroring is the basis for attunement and without this we cannot always develop accurate attunement with ourselves.

Empathy develops in response to being accurately seen and heard. I learn what to call my feeling because someone notices that I am having a feeling and says, "Are you tired, honey? Are you angry? Are your feelings hurt?" We learn to associate our physical and emotional feelings with a vocabulary word. If we were not seen and heard accurately, we may not have learned how to read ourselves and others as well as we think we can. In fact, we may often see their emotions and responses as more threatening than they are and we are unsure how to respond. For example, we worry that people are "angry" at us, not able to tell the difference between frustration, irritation or fatigue. We're usually too scared to ask them, afraid of the answer. Instead, we just act towards them as though they are angry with us, and we move into a placating mode that can be irritating to the other person. Then they really ARE irritated with us. We don't see it's a result of something WE are doing.

Matthew learned early in life that the way to stay under the radar and out of trouble was to guess what people needed and give it to them without being asked. When he would guess incorrectly as a child, he would be screamed at or hit, so he learned to pay very close attention to other people. However, he was never given any information about the inside world of the people in his family so he had no access to what they really might be feeling and thinking. He had to guess based on what they were doing. As a colleague, Tom has a tendency to watch his colleagues and adjust his workflow based on what he thinks is going to work best for them. For example, he will not use the computer when he needs to, assuming that his co-worker will want to do their progress reports right away after group. As a result, he was recently written up by his supervisor for being late with his assessments after his supervisor was dinged in an audit.

Matthew, like a lot of codependents, makes his decisions based on assumptions and doesn't give the other person a chance to weigh in or participate. He decides what they need for them, and as result wound up putting his supervisor in a bad position. It is our role to anticipate the needs of others (earning our value) and more often than not, others have no way to express their love to us by taking care of us. What if they find out we are "needy?" What if I find out I am "needy?"

Darla works incredibly hard at the treatment center. She volunteers for extra shifts and is willing to do things other counselors avoid like taking clients to an outside meeting or the doctor when she notices her co-workers seem to have a lot of work to do. In fact, Darla is so competent and "thoughtful" that when her family offers to help around the house and loads the dishwasher, she will come up behind them and re-arrange the dishwasher later. If she realizes they need a dentist appointment she is quick to step in to make one and then tell them when they have to show up for the appointment. Darla describes herself as helpful though eventually her resentment erupts when she becomes tired and annoyed at the unequal workload both at home and work. She has no idea how often she communicates that other people are incompetent and that she has TRAINED them not to participate. She jokingly says things like, "I know them better than they know themselves." She feels bad later when she has a tantrum in her resentment, gets really pissy or even gives her colleagues the silent treatment without telling them why.

If you begin to see that your behavior is intrusive at times or not considerate of those in your life, it's possible that you have operated in the world as though you were invisible because significant attachment figures did not notice your needs and wants. You simply addressed them yourself without checking in with others or working cooperatively. Maybe it was your experience that you would have to "take" what you needed regardless of the feelings of others because either significant attachment figures did not respond to your needs in a timely manner, or did not meet your needs appropriately.

It's also possible that you were expected to accurately "guess" the needs and wants of your caretakers, so you never learned social skills like "asking" people about their preferences. You were supposed to figure it out or you would be shamed or even threatened. So you operate largely on assumptions about the needs and wants of those you love and act towards them accordingly.

You will need to monitor your shame when you notice things about you that may be embarrassing or seem immature. We have pockets of responses that are "immature" because we didn't have the secure attachment bases from which to experiment with behaviors and try out alternative responses.

Instead, we mastered a defense or an "all-purpose" response to situations because we hadn't developed awareness of the full range of available emotions, thoughts, and behaviors. It is a "learning" issue, not a "character" issue. As we develop a stronger sense of "self" and a solid internal observer, we trust our impressions of others more and can tune into ourselves to pick up the unspoken agendas and feelings of others.

Symptom Three: Distrusting the Attachment of Others to the Codependent

Whether we are anxious about potential abandonment or refuse to connect to avoid the inevitable abandonment, we are often way too defensive to notice or trust the stated attachment of others to us. Even when people tell us they love us and are committed to us, we are always factoring in a "plan B."

People who are anxious or distrusting of attachment suspect that others don't value us as much as we value them. We're suspicious because we're over-giving, and others can't match our participation level. When we notice the discrepancy between our giving levels and the giving of others, we can develop resentments. We can interpret the imbalance as further proof that we are not "worthy" of being taken care of. It is proof of our foundational unloveability. We are highly alert to signs of disconnection, believing we can be easily replaced if we are not highly aware of the other person's needs. *If I fail to meet your needs promptly, even if it means sacrificing my own, you will simply find someone else who can do so.* After all, if you had a "choice" about attaching to me, you might not make that choice.

We spend a lot of time proving our worth, including super-hero levels of problem-solving hoping to solidify the attachment.

Larry hears it when his colleagues thank him for something he's done or when they acknowledge a really good intervention during group. However, Larry also learned early in life that love is highly conditional and what has been given can also be taken away. Despite evidence that his colleagues value him, Larry will still go above and beyond to "earn" his place on the team. He always takes the hardest, most resistant clients or works with the probation officer with the biggest attitude. One night one Larry discovered that one of the co-occurring clients had been "cheeking" his psych meds for the last four days. He also realized the client was decompensating when he began to accuse another client of trying to plant drugs in his room and listen to him through the television. Despite the client's agitation and history of violence when feeling backed into a corner, Larry decides it's too dangerous to let his co-worker handle the situation and that it would be best for him to put himself physically between the decompensating client and the client he was accusing. Moving forward prompts a fearful response from the agitated client who grabs a lamp and hits Larry over the head, knocking him out. Meanwhile, his co-worker has called the emergency responders and when they arrive they have to contain the client AND take care of Larry.

Larry is always taking one for the team, never feeling like he can trust that he's done enough. Instead of working with his co-worker as a team, he put on his hero cape and made the situation worse. Larry has no idea how often his co-workers feel vaguely guilty as a result of all of his over-work, knowing that he is doing more than his share. In truth, they would like and trust him even more if he was willing to be part of the team instead of doing everything himself. Their lack of trust would be a shocking revelation to Larry.

Sandra has been anxious to try a new group format at the treatment center after she attended a recent training. She has come back from the training full of thoughts about ways they could increase client retention and make groups more interesting. While Sandra's supervisor responds positively and has given her the go-ahead to write up her ideas, Sandra continues to monitor him, looking for signs that he's going to change his mind and give the project to her co-worker. As a result, she's dragging her feet on the write-up and wondering if she should find a back-up place to do her groups with another agency "just in case." As Sandra's supervisor notices her hesitation, he figures that she isn't as interested in moving forward as he thought and stops planning to move ahead. When he doesn't ask Sandra about the project, she concludes that she's been "dismissed" as usual and feels defeated.

We need to catch ourselves if we set up "tests" for people to prove to ourselves or them what they are "really" thinking. This kind of perspective creates an invisible barrier in relationships — it is almost impossible to be intimate with someone who is waiting for you to fail or waiting to "catch you" in a lie. In this case the lie is, "See, I knew you were full of shit when you said you loved me." While it is painful to "prove" that they don't love us, it does remove the anxiety of not being "sure" or waiting for abandonment.

We also need to check our motives when we find ourselves volunteering to do tasks for others, or get busy in activities designed to distract ourselves from our anxiety about the "truth" of others' attachment to us. Monitoring our thoughts, feelings, bodies and behavioral cues can give us insight into our motives.

Symptom Four: Escalation to Protect Attachment

When we feel that someone connected to us is becoming unavailable or not responding to us, we create scenes and drama to get the other person to take us seriously. When we suspect that someone connected to us is becoming unavailable or not responding to us, we create scenes by alternating dramatic angry demands with needy dependence. When they are preoccupied and not paying attention, the codependent explodes in angry demands and behaviors that cannot be ignored. It may have been a highly necessary strategy as a child — the only available option to capture the attention of a depressed or emotionally absent parent. It's a strategy that is no longer effective or useful in our adult relationships.

Monica is a hard working member of her treatment team. Despite being a seasoned professional with increased education, she is finding it very hard to transfer to the next open code in the county system. While she interviews well, Monica has a history of conflicts with management and co-workers that follows her. When she doesn't receive the recognition she feels she deserves, or feels disrespected by a non-responsive co-worker, she becomes belligerent and verbally aggressive. On more than one occasion she has threatened to file union complaints against a supervisor. Once she has "had her say" Monica feels resolved and moves on, not registering the long-term effects on her career. She expects her hard work outweighs her "occasional" mood swings.

Monica's inability to self-soothe and regulate her emotions creates a need for external calming solutions. This inability creates vulnerability to substance abuse to address her emotional distress. It is not unusual for her to spend an entire weekend Netflix binge-watching or eating 5,000 calories at once after a conflict with a co-worker. Monica is vulnerable to prescription pain medication addiction should she have surgery or dental work.

"Lack of moderate" is one of the most obvious signs of codependency to others. ***Moderation is essentially a self-containment issue and is related to both boundary and reality issues***. When an individual contains himself with a wall, he tends to shut down and wall others out. In this process, he loses control of being in control of himself and others.

Marcus comes from a long-line of gang-bangers and left the gang during his last incarceration to be available for his two-year-old son in a way his father had not been. He has three years clean and sober, and the recovery program is his first "legit" job. Accustomed to power through fear, Marcus is afraid of his potential to "lose it" and often finds his neck hurting and head aching after work because he spends so much energy not opening his "big mouth." Sometimes in a staff meeting he can feel his stomach knot up when the clinical supervisor doesn't address his concerns, a coworker drops the ball on one of Marcus' clients, or Marcus feels like his time is being "wasted." While he learned in prison to stay quiet, his coworkers find themselves avoiding him afterward due to the anger force field around him.

Codependents frequently don't trust the attachment when we perceive there to be a physical or emotional absence. We believe "out of sight, out of mind." Strong statements of our presence are called for, which could include stalking behaviors, tantruming, throwing scenes, obsessive calling, hacking into other's e-mail, etc. A moderate response never quite seems enough.

This particular symptom of codependency requires skills for emotional regulation and management. We are up against our almost instinctive hyper-response to perceived threats, which is physiological as well as emotional. Our heart begins to race, our thoughts race, we get warm and physically restless. This level of anxiety is hard to tolerate, and **doing something, anything,** can seem preferable to sitting still with this level of arousal.

So, we make calls we regret, make asses of ourselves and say things we don't mean. All in an attempt to discharge a painful level of arousal that makes us feel like we are coming out of our skin.

Half the battle with this pattern is to recognize that we are not behaving this way because someone is "making" us react this way. We are truly in control of our behaviors and have options in how to express our feelings. We have to make the decision to not abandon ourselves and remain accountable for what comes out of our mouths as well as our effect on others.

One of the best therapies around to manage this reactivity is called dialectical behavioral therapy (DBT). Multiple books have been written that outline this approach very well, especially those written by Marsha Linehan, Ph.D. Two particular concepts, mindfulness and primary/secondary emotions, are relevant to our discussion here.

One of the techniques DBT teaches to regulate and tolerate difficult emotions in **mindfulness.** It is different than meditation in that you don't "clear" your mind. The goal is to learn to watch your thoughts as they pass through your mind without getting attached or stuck on one particular emotion or thoughts. The technique is designed to teach you to observe your thoughts without judgment. This leads us to the second concept.

Primary/secondary emotions: the true source of our misery is caused by the secondary emotion happens when we judge our primary emotion. Dr. Linehan has observed that we all have our immediate emotional response to events, such as fear or anger, or excitement. However, we immediately judge these thoughts as good or bad, and proceed to have feelings about our first feeling or thought.

My first feeling might have been sadness but my immediate next thought is judgment about having this feeling: "That's a stupid thing to be sad about. Don't be such a cry baby." Then I feel shame about feeling sad. Dr. Linehan says that the true source of our misery is caused by the secondary emotion, which is the result of our judgment about the primary emotion. It is her observation that if we could feel the primary emotion and notice it without then labeling it or judging it, it will pass through much more rapidly and our distress would pass more quickly.

Closely connected to noticing emotions is noticing your self-talk about your emotions and the world around you. Much of our emotional response is driven by our interpretation of events outside of us. For example, if my husband is running late from work and has not called I have choices about how to interpret that FACT.

- "He's running late because he is avoiding me." = angry, hurt, anxious about the attachment

- "He's running late because I am not important to him. Screw him." = defensive, avoidant, angry

- "He's running later because it is the end of the quarter and he always has more workload at this time." = neutral emotions, compassion, not taking it personally

We have full choice on how to interpret the FACT that he is running late. We also have the choice to check-out our theory when he does get home.

Instead, we will often match our emotions to our theory and "act as if" our theory is true. So, by the time he does get home, we are in full emotional reactivity. We may even create a self-fulfilling prophecy as a result of directing so much negativity at him that he doesn't want to come home or stops caring about us. At which point we tell ourselves, "I knew it."

The more often we can draw neutral conclusions and recognize how seldom other people's thoughts and behaviors are about us; we can begin to react more accurately internally and therefore, externally. We will make fewer amends and apologies for jumping to conclusions, and feel more self-respect and self-control.

Symptom Five: Denial of Dependency or Attachment Needs

We use protective strategies so that we stay unaware of our needs for others, making sure that we don't get "too attached" so it won't hurt so much when they leave.

It's important in childhood to be able to return to our attachment figure for comfort when we feel threat or discomfort. For some codependents, the caregiver was most likely not able or was unwilling to consistently comfort. They may have even been punishing when comfort was requested.

We become fiercely self-reliant to avoid the pain of neglect or non-responsiveness.

Ted has been managing the chemical dependency unit for the last ten years and was the lead counselor five years before that. He is well respected and skilled. However, upper management has noticed that he seems unable to keep his lead counselors for more than a year or two before they transfer to another treatment site. They decide to do a 360-degree review for all managers to see if they can determine the problem. When they review the results, it becomes clear that Ted has a strong micro-management style. He does not share authority or control well and expects to "weigh-in" on every clinical decision. In fact, his team is very anxious overall and unwilling to grow clinically. The talented members begin to look for a way out while the passive, less ambitious members of the team remain.

Ultimately, Ted has become his own secure base, distrusting the capacity of others to meet his needs or respond in a competent or timely manner. Unfortunately, he has created an oppressive work environment to match his own less-than-nurturing view of the world. He would just say he is a "professional" and people's personal issues should not be present in the workplace.

Codependents can become counter dependent — if I can't provide the need for myself, then I will do without. We will not risk the possible rejection or non-response when asking for help. If we are forced into accepting assistance, we will feel obligated to return the help ten-fold. We assume assistance always comes with strings attached and we are unwilling to be placed in such a vulnerable position. It is unacceptable to "need" others in any tangible, structural way.

We allow ourselves to love and be loved, but not enough to entrust our security or share our position as our own "secure base." Childhood experience taught us that this was not wise and we may feel lonely at times, but we are unwilling to trade full participation at every level in order to reduce this loneliness.

Janice is the weekend family counselor, who is the backbone of the treatment unit. Family participation in the program is high and her reputation in the community is stellar. The program is lucky to have her. There are times when Janice feels overwhelmed with the calls she has to make and return and appointments that family members request that keep her well after her shift is over. When she thinks about taking time off she becomes anxious and worries that other staff members don't have the same relationship with the families and that the families then might feel abandoned. While she would like to have her own family someday, she can't see a realistic way to make that happen. Besides, chances are it would end like most marriages do and she'd go through what her mom went through. These people "need" her, and she tells herself that she can't have it all. God has called her to "service." She comforts herself with her four cats.

Both anxious and avoidant codependents deny their dependency needs to prepare for the eventual broken attachment. Because we do not trust our attachments or the attachments of others to us, we try to never put ourselves in a position to "need" a secure-based response from someone else.

We are terrified of the feelings that come with abandonment and have a variety of defenses in place to keep us from being open to that kind of pain. This fear doesn't mean that codependents don't get attached or love, it simply means that we are vigilant for the possible, if not inevitable, point in time when the attachment will not continue or be strong enough to support us when we most need it.

There may well come a time when our attachment figures will decide that our needs and wants are "too much" and withdraw their willingness to provide a secure base from which we operate. Therefore, we need always to hold something back in reserve, much like a secret bank account which we operate.

If I don't trust my ability to be resilient in the face of distress, I am certainly not going to be willing to allow its possibility.

The idea is to allow ourselves to soften some of our hard edges. It requires us to take the risk of "needing" someone for support and consistent response. We have to see someone or something outside of ourselves as a possible "secure base" where we can return if we get hurt or need guidance. It means to allow other people to be part of the solution.

Symptom Six: Avoiding Intimacy

When we talk about mattering, we are entering into the intimacy territory, a tough place for anxious and avoidant codependents. If you have been working on attunement with yourself and emotional regulations skills, you will have an easier time in this area. You will know more about yourself and have more to share at an intimate level. What does intimacy mean?

> *It means to allow someone to see you as you are, without masks or illusions. It means that you are consistently yourself regardless of the situation. What you see is what you get – so you are congruent emotionally, intellectually and behaviorally. There's no pretense.*

We are often highly available to others, careful to not "overburden" others with our issues so that we avoid allowing ourselves to express a "need" for comfort from people who may fail us or be unresponsive. Anne Wilson Schaef refers to this as impression management, where we will invest a great deal of energy into managing other's feelings and impressions of us. If we were honest with ourselves, very few people actually "know us" at an intimate level, though they may have the impression they are closer to use than they are.

Karla grew up dodging the running commentary from her alcoholic father who described her as "lazy," "half-witted" and "useless." She drives herself mercilessly to prove him wrong. She is incredibly judgmental of anyone on the treatment team, or even on her caseload, that SHE decides is lazy or doesn't have her commitment to recovery. After all, she stayed clean the FIRST time once her prescription pill addiction was identified. Karla is the program manager for a large private facility and often provides public workshops, which makes her visible and well known in her community. She's outgoing, communicative and appears emotionally available. No one knows how much time she spends alone and how much energy "looking competent" takes from her.

Many of us have been shamed about human imperfections, having been incorrectly taught that making mistakes is terrible, shameful and completely unacceptable. We are "supposed" to know things without having to ask or without being told. Letting someone see us in our imperfection would guarantee abandonment and broken attachment, right? Karla is completely convinced of this, which is why people may think they know her but only the "her" she wants them to see.

The famous psychoanalyst Carl Jung introduced the concept of "the shadow" to describe the parts of ourselves that we push away or deny because we believe them to be unacceptable. They are qualities we see in others that we hate or irritate us and that we judge harshly.

We use a great deal of energy to deny to ourselves and others that we possess these qualities, "I'm not a jealous person — I don't have a jealous bone in my body," or "I'm never angry, I just don't understand angry people," or "I am happiest making others happy, I can't stand selfish people." Somewhere along the way we learned that having these qualities can result in abandonment and broken attachments, and we insist that these qualities can't be true of us. If we do see them, we feel deeply ashamed and we are very afraid other people will find out they are true of us. Others knowing our "shadow" can make us very anxious.

Donna recognizes that she has a tendency to get "too involved" with her clients and worries about them even when her shift is over. She is the oldest of three sisters with a depressed and unavailable Mom. She also spent a lot of time protecting her mom and sisters from their violent father. She is the only one who could stand up to him — she is most like him although she would completely deny this. At her performance review, her clinical supervisor comments on her over-involvement in her cases, observing that she takes their treatment success or failure too personally. He also says there have been complaints that she's intimidating to clients, and co-workers she perceives to be "picking" on her clients. Donna is shocked at this, quickly stating that she "hates" bullies and would NEVER use intimidation tactics like her father did. She believes the other counselors just don't have her passion for the work and want her to "phone it in" like they do.

The more of the shadow qualities that I possess, the more guarded I will be against intimacy. I will keep the door on the closet locked pretty tight. However, Jung said we do this in vain because these qualities will leak out of our unconscious. Certainly Donna would be horrified if she could see herself the way her co-workers do. She has spent a lifetime denying any connection to her father, not realizing that the same bullying qualities her co-workers see were necessary strengths in her childhood. She needs to see the strategy as outdated, not a character stain.

Carl Jung pointed out that the path to healing this was to accept all aspects of ourselves, the "good" and "bad" instead of attempting to compartmentalize and discard aspects of ourselves. These aspects are all part of being human and if we can acknowledge them, we will be more in control of their presence in our lives.

Symptom Seven: Walls Instead of Boundaries

We have to learn the difference between walls and boundaries. Pia Melody points out that boundaries serve two primary functions: **protecting us from the intrusion of others and containing our intrusive behaviors**. When we looked at the lack of attunement with others, it seemed clear that my obliviousness to my impact on other people could lead me to offend them or invade their internal or external boundaries without knowing it. I could tell them how they "should" feel, because their fear or anger makes ME anxious or uncomfortable. I could do their laundry to "help" without asking if they would be okay with me sorting through their personal items.

JJorge spent the last two years of his incarceration focused on starting his life over. He was tired of being incarcerated and recognized that meth was going to keep taking him there. He enrolled in every program the prison offered and worked hard. Jorge has a love for incarcerated people, believing he can bring his experience and willingness to change to help people like himself. He completed his addiction studies program and had been working with ex-offenders for the last three years. He is so committed to making a difference that his co-workers notice that he almost seems aggressive in staff meetings. He feels like he needs to "advocate" for HIS people whenever the staff want to apply consequences due to program rule violations. He has even "overlooked" a few dirty tests, identifying that everyone needs a second chance. He doesn't want to give up his clients like everyone else has. The staff has noticed that his office mate, Adrian, seems to be almost afraid of Jorge, and defers to his demands for his clients because Jorge seems to "care" so much.

Adrian could allow intrusive behavior from Jorge because of her lack of attunement with herself. She would not recognize that she is uncomfortable until later and then she may not connect her anxiety with the earlier boundary invasion.

One of the goals of therapy is to feel our feelings in "real-time" without this delayed reaction phenomenon. The sooner I recognize what is going on inside of me, the sooner I can take care of myself or the situation.

When I do not trust my ability to make good judgments, or trust my ability to be accurately attuned to myself and others, I HAVE to have walls to protect me. We don't need walls because other people aren't safe. We need them because we can't tell the difference between the good guys and the bad guys and so we keep everyone out just to be sure.

Veronica wants badly to be taken seriously by the treatment team. She has never held a "real" job before going to school because she was taking care of her two kids while her husband traveled on his job until he left her last year. She sees herself as "lucky" that someone would hire her. Veronica's husband always pointed out that she doesn't seem to have any "sense" when it comes to seeing people as they are, and teased her about her gullibility. Acutely aware of this "thing" about her, she decides to take a watchful and observing position, figuring that she doesn't know how what's really going on. So, she works overtime, and her work is perfect. However, she contributes almost nothing at staff meetings, and her coworkers have learned not to rely on her because they can't get a "read" on her. Veronica can feel this and assumes that they see her as "weak" which makes her share even less about herself. It's a terrible cycle.

Lack of attunement with other's agendas, needs and feelings can make the world around us seem very confusing. We will either stay under the radar, like Veronica, or we will say, "I just don't play politics," or "I just tell it like it is. If you don't want to hear 'the truth' then don't ask me." Because we don't understand others, we will often take a position where we don't even try to connect or be tactful.

We give ourselves permission to just barrel though situations with a "take me or leave me" perspective that gives others very little room to maneuver or compromise with us. It's almost as though we expect others to work hard to get through our walls to prove they really love us. This is a lot to ask of other people.

Sarah sees herself as a "straight-shooter" and is proud of her willingness to tell it like it is. She sees most people as cowardly and will even state that she has "bigger balls" than the men on her team. She is fearless on behalf of her treatment team and other managers at her level know better than to come into conflict with her. Sarah describes herself as an activist and has no idea that her colleagues have coffee without her because including her creates more difficulty than it's worth. They get tired of her defensiveness and the truth is, her team does miss out on opportunities due to the perception of Sarah as more trouble than she's worth.

There are different kinds of walls we use to create a safe bubble for ourselves:

- Silence
- Anger
- Loaded
- Inept
- Righteous
- Depression
- Busyness
- Confusion
- Hysterical
- Too Nice
- Judgmental

Carlos is well-loved on the treatment unit. He's kind, patient and incredibly level-headed. No-one ever has a conflict with Carlos, as he is quick to defer to other's strong preferences. His philosophy is "How important is it?" and if you were watching him, you would conclude it NEVER matters. This philosophy became evident recently when the staff wanted to celebrate his eighth recovery birthday, and were trying to figure out how to honor him. As they discuss it amongst themselves, it becomes clear that no one is sure what his favorite cake is, what he does on his free time or what hobbies he has. Everyone realizes that despite the feeling that they "love Carlos to pieces," there is a lot about him that they don't know.

The key to healing this aspect of our codependency will be to identify the various strategies we use to create intimacy barriers in our relationships with others. This can be challenging because we have been using these strategies for so long that we have come to believe, "this is the way I am" — we don't see them as behaviors but see them as our character.

Due to the long-term presence of these walls, we may need to get outside input to see ourselves accurately. We can ask people we trust to give us feedback about their first impressions of us. We can ask family members to point out our walls when they go up and we can be open to the feedback even if it's uncomfortable. Remember that you cannot change behavior that you cannot see.

Chapter Three

Physiology of the Stress Response Connected to Codependency

Ultimately, codependency is a chronic stress disease that can devastate our immune system and lead to systemic and even life-threatening illness.

Attachment issues set the emotional and developmental stage for future behaviors. The fight or freeze response is the physical mechanism that leads to our physical deterioration and lowered immune system. The fight, flight or freeze response prepares us to respond in an emergency.

Attachment Implications in Developing Chronic Illness

Attachment insecurity leads to disease risk through three mechanisms:

- Increased susceptibility to stress: anxious and avoidant codependents struggle with emotional regulation and reactivity, even if it is only internal, and often find themselves in stressful interpersonal situations that trigger overwhelming physical flooding.

- Increased use of external regulators of affect: anxious people will engage in stressful interpersonal attempts to self-soothe or the use of substances that escalate their anxiety while avoidant codependents are more vulnerable to the use of alcohol, work, and isolation to manage their internal distress.

- Altered help-seeking behavior: anxious codependents will overuse medical professionals and others in an attempt to engage the stress that seems to flood them and feels out of control to them. This increased engagement makes them vulnerable to medication abuse. Avoidant codependents are less likely to seek help and allow themselves to become more acutely ill with greater physical consequences as they avoid asking for help or support.

Attachment insecurity contributes to physical illness through increased susceptibility to stress.

Isolation can affect our physical health. For example, well-designed studies have shown that a small social network or inadequate emotional support is association with a threefold increase in subsequent cardiac events among patients who have already had a heart attack, and a two-to-threefold increase in future coronary artery disease among healthy patients. In fact, Robert Sapolsky has found the effect of social support on life expectancy may be as strong as the effects of obesity, cigarette-smoking, hypertension, or level of activity.

Barbara struggles to make ends meet with her full-time job at the treatment center, and decides to take on extra work at the DUI agency. She is primarily concerned with her 15-year-old son who has been expelled again. She is frantic with worry that he will turn out "just like his father" who has been incarcerated for the last year. However, she is even more afraid that her co-workers will find out that she doesn't have her "shit" together, and think she shouldn't be working with clients if she can't even manage her home life. Truthfully, Barbara suspects this is probably right. No one at work has any idea that Barbara is managing this level of stress, nor that she has started taking Tagamet to manage her almost constant heartburn. She can't afford to take time off — she is the only financial support for her family.

Adverse Childhood Experiences Study

The ACE study shows a clear scientific link between many types of childhood adversity, and adult onset of physical diseases and mental health disorders:

- Verbal put down and humiliation

- Emotionally and physically neglected

- Physically or sexually abused

- Living with a depressed parent, a parent with mental illness, a parent addicted to alcohol or drugs

- Witnessing a mother being abused

- Losing a parent to separation or divorce

The key is that they are scary and UNPREDICTABLE stressors.

17,000 people took the ACE to help the researchers understand how childhood events might affect adult health. The patients that ACE researchers Felitti and Anda surveyed were not troubled or disadvantaged.

The average patient was 57 years old and three out of four were college educated. They were successful men and women with good educations, mostly white, middle class, with health benefits and stable jobs.

- 64% answered yes to one or more category.

- 87% of those who answered yes to one ACE question had additional ACE questions.

- 40% had experienced two or more categories of ACE.

- 12.5% had an ACE score of four or more.

- 1/3 had a score of zero.

How many categories of ACE patients had encountered would, by and large, predict how much medical care they would require in adulthood. The higher one's ACE score, the higher the number of doctor visits they'd had in the past year and the higher their number of unexplained health symptoms.

People with a score of four or more were twice as likely to be diagnosed with cancer as someone with a zero. For each ACE score, an individual had, the chance of being hospitalized with and autoimmune disease in adulthood rose 20 percent. Someone with an ACE score of four was 400 percent more likely to be facing depression than someone with a score of zero. An ACE score of six or more shortened an individual's lifespan by almost 20 years.

These types of chronic adversities change the architecture of the brain, altering the expression of genes that control stress hormone output. Hormone output triggers an overactive inflammatory stress response for life and predisposes the child to adult disease.

Debbie learned early in life to check out of her needs and wants as the child of a bi-Polar mother and absent father. Debbie was the middle of three siblings, and felt it was important not to give her erratic mother any further stress, especially since her older brother was a "handful." She managed herself and her younger sister, who to this day calls Barbara "Mom." Debbie is a smart, resourceful woman and participates as much in her children's life as she possibly can with her schedule. She knows it is not enough, and when she watches her oldest son struggle, she feels hopeless. Debbie's father died in his 50's of his alcoholism, and she believes she will avoid this by not drinking. She is unaware of the deadly toll her life stress is taking on her.

Scientists at Duke, UC San Francisco and Brown have shown that childhood adversity damages us at a cellular level in ways that prematurely age our cells and affect our longevity. Adults who faced early life stressors show greater erosion in telomeres — which are protective caps that sit on the ends of strands of DNA to keep DNA healthy and intact. As telomeres erode, we are more likely to develop disease and age faster.

Stephen Porges writes in his polyvagal theory about the importance of autonomic systems and the ventral-vagal complex to the regulation of emotions. The vagus nerve is a primary nerve of the parasympathetic nervous system and helps people self-regulate and seek out and use the help of others to regulate and engage in non-threatening moments. Porges suggest that human beings have evolved a hierarchically organized series of responses to threat. In what is, in fact, the third but highest level of response (i.e. most evolved and newest), the organism engages the ventral-vagal system, which is responsible for signaling others in the environment regarding movement and emotion through its control over facial expressions and vocalization. Porges refers to this as the "social engagement system."

The Theory of Everything

The immune system is the body's master operating control system. What happens in the brain in childhood sets up a lifelong programming for this master operating system governing all: body, brain and mind.

The unifying principle of this new "theory of everything" is this: your emotional biography becomes your physical biology, and together they write much of the script for how you will live your life.

"Our findings showed that the ten different types of adversity we examined were almost equal in their damage," says Felitti. This was true even though some types, such as sexual abuse, are more shameful in our society.

Normal Stress Response

Stephen Porges writes in his polyvagal theory about the importance of autonomic systems and the ventral-vagal complex to the regulation of emotions. The vagus nerve is a primary nerve of the parasympathetic nervous system and helps people self-regulate and seek and use the help of others to regulate and engage in non-threatening moments. Porges suggest that human beings have evolved a hierarchically organized series of responses to threat. In what it, in fact, the third but highest level of response (i.e. most evolved and newest), the organism engages the ventral-vagal system, which is responsible for signaling others in the environment regarding movement and emotion through its control over facial expressions and vocalization. Porges refers to this as the "social engagement system."

When this strategy fails, humans revert to an older system, the sympathetic nervous system, which was adapted to mobilize fight or flight response strategies. If that is not sufficient to avert the stress, threat, danger, or attack, we rely on our earliest adapted stress response, which uses the dorsal vagal system to immobilize the body engaging in a freezing response and even feigning death

Let's say you are lying in bed and everyone else in the house is asleep. It's 1 a.m. You hear a creak on the steps. Then another creak. Now it sounds as though there is someone is in the hallway. You feel a sudden rush of alertness — even before your conscious mind weighs the possibilities of what might be going on. A small region in your brain known as the hypothalamus releases hormones that stimulate two little glands — the pituitary and the adrenal glands — to pump chemicals throughout your body.

(Sympathetic Nervous Responses – Fight or Flight) Adrenaline and cortisol trigger immune cells to secrete powerful messenger molecules that whip up your body's immune response. Your pulse drums under your skin as you lie there, listening. The hair on the surface of your arms stands up. Muscles tighten. Your body gets charged up to do battle in order to protect life and limb.

HYPERVIGILANCE tunes out all information except immediate threat.

Then you recognize those footsteps as those of your teenager coming up the steps after finishing his midnight bowl of cereal. He pops his head in, sees your face, and says, "It's all good, mom." **(Parasympathetic Response)** *Your body relaxes. Your muscles loosen. The hair on your arms flattens back down. Your hypothalamus, as well as your pituitary and adrenal glands, the HPA stress axis, calm down.*

After the stressful event, your body dampens down the fight–or-flight response. Your system recovers and returns to a baseline state of rest and recovery.

The parasympathetic system is key to regulating our emotional distress. Our facial expression, tone of voice, body language all are right brain indicators of information and critical components of what Dan Seigel refers to as "interpersonal neurobiology," our brain's capacity to affect and be affected by other's brains. It is key to our healing that we have others in our lives that can see and respond to these signals.

If you are not able to engage your parasympathetic system, then the dorsal vagal system kicks in:

Dissociation (Freeze)

Dissociation due to threat and/or trauma may involve:

- Distorted sense of time.

- A detached feeling that you are observing something happen to you as if it is unreal — the sense that you may be watching a movie of your life.

- In extreme cases, children may withdraw into an elaborate fantasy world where they may assume special powers or strengths.

For most children and adults the adaptive response to an acute trauma involves a mixture of hyperarousal and dissociation. "Leaving the body" is the body's survival mechanism and in lesser states can be seen in day-dreaming. In trauma, we have this protective mechanism triggered automatically, and we lose control over our ability to stay present in the face of something that frightens us, even as adults.

Normal immune system

Lets' say your immune system has to fight a viral or bacterial infection. Lots of white blood cells charge to the site of the infection. Those white blood cells secrete inflammatory cytokines to help destroy the infiltrating pathogens and repair damaged tissues. However, when those cytokines aren't well regulated, or become too great in number, rather than repair tissue they cause tissue damage.

Emotions create the same response

When we experience stressful emotions — anger, fear, worry, anxiety, rumination, grief, loss — the HPA axis releases stress hormones, including cortisol and inflammatory cytokines, that promote inflammation.

Although humans are designed to rebound from high-intensity survival states, we also have the problematic ability to neo-cortically override the discharge of excess survival energy. Through rationalizations, judgments, shame, enculturation, and fear of our bodily sensations, we may disrupt our innate capacity to self-regulate, functionally "recycling" disabling terror and helplessness. When the nervous system does not reset after an overwhelming experience, sleep, cardiac, digestion, respiration, and immune system function can be seriously disturbed. Unresolved physiological distress can also lead to an array of other physical, cognitive, emotional, and behavioral symptoms.

More subtle types of tissue damage can happen slowly over time, in response to chronic stress. When your system is repeatedly overstimulated, it begins to downshift in response to stress. On the face of it, that might sound like a good thing — as if a downshifted stress response should translate into less inflammation, right?

But remember, this stress response is supposed to react to a big stressor, pump into defensive action, quickly recover and then return to a state of quiet homeostasis, relaxing into rest and recovery. **The problem is, when you are facing a lot of chronic stress, the stress response never shuts off.** You're caught, perpetually, in the first half of the stress cycle. There is no state of recovery. Instead, the stress response is always mildly on — pumping out a chronic low dose of inflammatory chemicals. The stress glands, the hypothalamus, the HPA axis, secrete low levels of stress hormones all the time leading to chronic cytokine activity and inflammation.

Lou has lived his life in chaos as long as he can remember. He would be sent in the evening by his mom to get his dad at the bar because his dad would be too drunk to drive home safely. He would manage his feelings as he watched his dad stagger out of the bar and wondered about the other men there. Did their sons come and get them? However, this was normal, and it didn't occur to him it could be any other way. As a result, Lou learned to drink to bond with his dad pretty early in life, and it worked pretty well for a long time. Then Lou started racking up consequences like DUI's and could no longer be the chauffeur, which created distance between himself and his dad. There was even more distance between them in Lou's sobriety. People who know him marvel that no matter what's going on Lou always seems to handle himself well, and it true that he is remarkably resilient . He manages his temper and just keeps moving forward. Now that's he's clean sober there isn't much outward difference. In fact, his life is even more stable and he seems to be a recovery success. Lou can't understand why he still can't get his blood pressure under control, even though he's not drinking and taking his medication. His doctor says he still has "stroke" levels of hypertension.

Simply

Chronic stress leads to dysregulation of our stress hormones, which leads to unregulated inflammation and inflammation translates into symptoms and disease.

This immune system impact is why there is a significant link between individuals who experience chronic stress and significantly higher levels of inflammation and disease.

Neurobiology of Attachment

Neurobiology, Dan Siegel states, explains that when we are "feeling felt" in early childhood, our dopamine system expands which results in allowing or wanting to "be seen." Conversely, he defines shame as simply the absence of attunement. Siegel goes on to purport that shame contracts the dopamine system and leads the child to attempt to be "unseen."

Alan Schore's research has shown that in the attuned moment between child and caregiver, both have that biological experience of the opiate system firing. These systems serve to reinforce the attachment and bond within the relationship. When people have healthy relationships, both the dopamine and opiate systems are sustained.

The body, limbic region, and cortex are involved in the physiological, emotional and intentional states as one person resonates within another who is paying attention to the other's facial expressions. As an attentive primary caregiver tunes into the needs of an infant, gazes into the infant's eye and meets its needs for affection, safety and sustenance; the infant tunes into the needs of an infant (himself), and gazes into the infant's eye (as reflected in the caregiver's eyes).

Social neuroscientists Heinrich and Lee have found that the hormone oxytocin plays an important role in social communication, affiliation, sexual behavior, trust, and anxiety reduction. Oxytocin has also been shown to improve one's ability to recognize a familiar face, to correctly classify a facial expression as either positive or negative, and to correctly infer the mental state of another person. It is also known that during states of fear or stress, oxytocin reduces anxiety by dampening the cortisol system (HPA axis) and inhibiting the amygdala and related sympathetic nervous system.

According to Ruth Buczynski, PhD and Ruth Lanius, MD, PhD, there are four primary deficits that result from damaged attachment: problems with emotional awareness, emotion regulation, self-referential processing and a stable sense of self.

Problems with **emotional awareness** indicates a disconnection from their inner emotional life; not knowing what they feel and not having a language to communicate their feelings. That often leads to a cascade of difficulties in relationships and in their ability to regulate their emotional states; they don't know what they are feeling.

Kevin finds himself sometimes confused in process group, especially when his clients seem all "emo" and he can't figure out why they are so upset. He feels compassion for them at first, but then he starts to get irritated and feels like he just wants to check out. His clients can feel it when Kevin isn't all there, and the other counselors are struggling because Kevin's clients come to them with issues, even when Kevin is on shift.

Emotional dysregulation means a codependent is on an emotional roller coaster. They feel like they have no control over their emotions — they actually feel controlled by their emotions. That can lead to a number of difficulties like substance abuse, people feel so overwhelmed by their emotions that they often turn to alcohol or street drugs in an attempt to regulate their emotions. People who have early life trauma can move back and forth between states of hyper-arousal and hypo-arousal, they don't necessarily get locked into one mode or the other. This creates an inner experience of a person who is being hijacked back and forth between those two modes — that would be very destabilizing and distressful for them.

Caroline sometimes wonders if she might be Bi-polar. Her co-workers wonder about this as well. Caroline can be a having a pretty good day, leading her groups well and getting paperwork done and then suddenly feel like she wants to slap her co-worker silly. It honestly feels like it comes out of the blue and it seems impossible for her to connect her reaction to what is happening between Caroline and her co-worker. Her coworkers are reluctant to do groups with her and avoid her in general, which hurts her feelings. Her clinical supervisor is thinking she is clearly not a team player and is thinking of letting her go.

Self-referential: codependents have tremendous difficulties interacting socially, and this is related to the concept of self-referential processing. People with early life trauma often see themselves as being worthless, broken, not worthy of being treated well and they expect the worst things to happen to them. They will probably find criticism, rejection, and abandonment in every interaction. Tales of depression, despair, fatigue, chronic anxiety and failure to achieve perfection will be commonplace in their personal stories.

Sylvia spends a lot of time talking to her sponsor about her co-workers and sometimes her clients. She sees herself as hard working and good at her job but feels like other people overlook her and even sabotage her at work. She's afraid to ask for input when she is stuck on a case because she thinks it might be used against her and as a result, does make obvious mistakes with her paperwork. When her clinical director brings it to Sylvia's attention, she quickly spirals into a shame attack and initially acts defensively. She then becomes tearful and fearful that she is going to be fired. Her reactivity makes giving Sylvia feedback very difficult, and her clinical supervisor always dreads having to meet with her.

The **sense of self** codependents often experience includes intense shame and guilt; their self is annihilated. This loss of self leads to poor boundaries and lack of an internal observer that recognizes our impact on other people. Lack of an internal observer leads to intrusiveness, poor recognition of social cues and even cognitive distortion. Codependents need to recognize and accept their actual competence and potential, so they can tolerate criticisms or failures.

Jack doesn't get his co-worker, Marsha, who seems to have "Dad" issues. When he wants to talk to her about a client she seem to get defensive and avoids him but he notices that she seems willing to talk to other people on the team. He wonders if she might feel intimidated by him because he has more experience. He has tried to be nice to her by offering to take her to lunch or even go to a movie. These invitations seem to make things worse, and he wonders if maybe she's just neurotic or something. He has no awareness that his behavior could be seen as sexual harassment.

Neurobiology of Love

When our brain is at rest, when nothing major is going on, when we are between intense feeling states, we are in a state of "idling" says Ruth Lanius, MD. When the brain is idling, a network of neurocircuitry, known as the brain's default mode network, quietly hums along like a car idling in the driveway. The areas of the brain in the default mode network include those associated with memory, those that help us construct thought, to recognize that others have thoughts and to help us as we integrate our thoughts. All those regions are integral to our internal thought process.

This network is always on standby, ready to help us figure out what we need to do next. "The dense connectivity in these areas of the brain help us determine what's relevant or not relevant so that we can be ready for whatever our environment is going to ask of us," says Lanius. "It is also integrally connected to areas of the brain that relate one's sense of self, one's feeling state."

This network helps us have an internal observer, the part of us that knows what we feel and think and sees our impact on those around us. We can get a realistic read on who we are and how others perceive us, which allows us to adjust our behavior when appropriate. It allows us to read the world around us accurately and be emotionally attuned.

People who have suffered trauma have very little connectivity in the default mode network. Their basic sense of self — who they are at the core when they are at rest or at peace. The brain seems not to have a healthy idling position – or to put it another way – equilibrium. Unpredictable chronic stressors of adverse childhood experience can hurt the neuroconnectivty in this part of the brain.

"Emotions become futile," says Lanius. "It would drive you crazy to be feeling a lot of emotions and yet to know you can't act on what you feel and so you become disassociated from your feeling state. **You become emotionally unaware of what's going on around you.**"

Years later, this freezing or shutting off has immense consequences for adult relationships. We may simply turn off unpleasant feelings, unable to respond with compassion for ourselves or others, or be turned off by anyone showing signs of neediness in general.

Karen really enjoys her time with the clients in the afternoon shift when the counselors are busy and as a CD tech, she can just "hang" with them. She would say she is relaxed and feels good about being part of the treatment team. The counselors worry when Karen is on shift because she tends to miss signs that tensions are brewing between clients or that a client may be isolating and not responding. She gets lost in conversation with a client while the others are left to manage themselves which is not a good thing in residential treatment. She doesn't seem able to manage a conversation and stay aware of what is going on around her and is always surprised when she learns that something took place on her shift. She thinks to herself, "Where was I?" which is the same question her supervisor will ask.

We might not recognize dangerous or unhealthy situations and interactions which in turn, allows us to enter or stay in relationships that are chaotic or harmful because they seem familiar and safe.

We may veer with little warning from a state of feeling to a state of heightened feeling. We may give too much in a relationship or to needy friends and family, because we're emotionally unattuned to our interior cues that should tell us we need to draw stronger boundaries — then we may erupt in anger when we realize that we're giving more than we're receiving.

Brains can show that individuals who lack emotional awareness have lost interconnected neurocircuitry in critical areas. The more emotionally unaware these individuals are, the less activation they show not only in the default mode network but also in an area of the brain known as the insula. The insula is a region involved in interoceptive awareness — **how aware we are of our bodily cues that tune us into what's happening to us at the moment.**

Lanius has also found that those who have a dampened sense of emotionality show less activity in an area of the cortex that indicates that they are not self-reflective, they are not aware of what they feel emotionally, nor are they able to reflect on it mindfully.

Stan's co-workers see him as thoughtful, quiet and even a little shy. In fact, becoming an addiction counselor is a surprising choice for Stan in some ways due to how many groups he will have to lead and the amount of normal chaos in residential treatment. Stan values his lack of reactivity, which is what he thinks makes him perfect for addiction work. He would say that his calmness is good for the clients and that he is a good balance for the reactive members of the staff. He is unaware that his lack of reactivity makes it hard for his co-workers to know what he's thinking and makes it hard for them to trust him. They are never quite sure if he has their back since they don't trust him to respond promptly.

This lack of awareness of feelings, this lack of consciousness as to how you might be contributing to disharmony or friction in a relationship presents a problem for partners and co-workers since the only way to manage your internal world is first to be aware of your internal reality. Without awareness, you can't be conscious of your behavior, and without consciousness of your behavior, you don't know how to improve your interactions in your most meaningful life experiences.

Lanius' MRI studies also show that trauma decreases activity in an area of the brain that affects our ability to regulate and modulate emotions. When we have difficulty regulating our emotions and rebounding from stress, we are more kindled into anger. We may overreact to what we perceive as rejection, or injustice or have a knee-jerk reaction to disagreements and discord. We may become hyper-aggressive, argumentative, defensive and angry. "When our emotions are under-regulated," explains Lanius. "This decreases our ability to dampen down intense feelings leading to greater activity in the amygdala, which regulates our emotional reactivity."

Robert has been taking care of himself since he ran away at 13 years old from his abusive home. He ran away from foster placements and despite his tough early life, he has managed to put himself through school and has created his own stable family. He believes this is possible because he is always in control. In fact, threats to his control in situations threatens Robert personally, something his co-workers could know very well. Robert is having difficulty getting through his internship and was asked to leave from his first placement site. His supervisor found him rigid and unwilling to take direction. After the first semester, his supervisor told him the placement was no longer working and that he would have to make arrangements for the second half of the course. Robert was furious and blamed the site for not giving him the training he needed to be successful. In his new placement. he figures he will have to "play politics" and get along until he gets his certification and then can do what he "damn well" needs to do.

Some of us over-modulate. Feeling so anxious and unable to process our feelings that we get quiet, we double-down, we passively retreat, and we avoid confrontation at all costs. We may feel overwhelmed by feelings of loss and betrayal.

Dan is the only boy of four children who was raised by a volatile and abusive mother. She believed that fear would keep the children in line, afraid they would turn out to be drunks like their dad. She was especially afraid for Dan and therefore was harshest towards him. She would lecture him for hours and he learned early on to pretend to listen to her while thinking his own thoughts instead of protesting. When he did try to stand up for himself, she would react with violence and then teach him a lesson by giving him the silent treatment because he obviously didn't want to hear what she had to say. Dan responds in a similar fashion on the treatment team. He has an enormously hard time with the assertive clients whom he sees as aggressive, and the rest of the staff gets frustrated because he seems incapable of following the structure if the client's push back. He claims it is because of "individualized treatment" goals but they rest of the staff knows he's conflict avoidant.

Role of attachment

When we grow up without secure attachments, we will not be wired for love. The woman who can't stop blaming her husband for every small infraction; the man who can't stop controlling his wife; their brains didn't receive the soothing they needed to foster the critical neuronal connections that create secure, loving attachments. They keep bumping up against the same neurobiological deficits over and over again.

Chapter Four

There is Hope

I have made an argument that codependency recovery requires us to address the developmental origins of our behaviors and pay attention to the physical consequences of long-term stressors caused by our distrust of the attachment in our relationships. I have passion about this because it kills us — it leads to stress and physical disability for addiction counselors and we need every counselor we have. We don't have enough well-trained, competent treatment professionals. We need you and your expertise. You spent years developing your skills and expertise, and it's important that you take care of you.

Biology is NOT Destiny

Experts tell us that **biology and childhood trauma are NOT destiny.**

We can reboot our brains, we can regain muscle tone, we can recover function in interconnected areas of the brain. The brain and body are never static; they are always in the process of becoming and changing. Researcher S. Cramer defines neuroplasticity as the ability of the nervous system to response to intrinsic or extrinsic stimuli by reorganizing its structure, function and connections. By repeatedly activating specific areas of the brain we can strengthen those areas.

Even if we have been set on high reactive mode for decades or a lifetime, we can still dial it down. We can respond to life's inevitable stressors more appropriately and shift away from an over-reactive inflammatory response; we can become neurobiologically resilient.

Wally has recently received feedback from his supervisor that he needs to "step it up," and be timelier in his responses to clients and co-workers. He seems to be avoiding things that might be uncomfortable, and it is leading to unresolved issues on the team. Wally has been working with a therapist to figure out what his "problem" is, and as they look further at his childhood, it becomes obvious that he doesn't trust himself or other people to not over-react in a conflict. In fact, he expects things to jump off and get out of control and as a result, has learned to shove aside any concerns he has. He tends to think people are yelling or more hostile than they are, (over-estimate the threat) and so he is beginning to practice taking breaths, timeouts, and check-ins with his sponsor to get reality checks when he feels like something is "too much." In the process, he is beginning to trust himself a little more to be more honest when he's in a staff meeting and has been pleased to see his co-workers talking to him more often. Who knew?

Resilient Wobble

Resilient people have what psychologists call "wobble" which is the ability to waver under the weight of life's suffering and trauma but not fall down.

Allostasis

Psychiatrists refer to the amount of trauma we experience over the course of our lives, and the cumulative effect of that trauma — how much wear and tear it takes on our body, brain and mind — as our "allostatic load." The term, coined by Bruce McEwen, Ph.D., is derived from allostasis, which is the ability to adapt over time to the stressful emotional and physical trials we encounter, return to a state of equilibrium and regain our sense of well-being. We wobble, we recover and we get on living our lives.

Upside of Adversity

Mark Seery, PhD, has been searching for the upside of adversity, asking whether some stress exposure might make people stronger over the long term. Seery had hundreds of patients who suffered from chronic, debilitating back pain complete a survey about their lifetime exposure to 37 different types of stressful experiences.

"Patients who had experienced absolutely no prior adversity in their childhood fared just as poorly as those who had experienced high levels of adversity," he says. In other words, those participants who had a score of zero on all childhood adversity questions — including the mild stressors Seery had included — were just as likely to be deeply disabled by their back pain and seek treatment for anxiety and depression, as were those who had experienced significant levels of adversity when they were young.

On the other hand, patients who have met some adversity when they were young, but not too much, were least likely to be disabled due to back pain later in life or seek later treatment for anxiety or depression.

Experiencing the right dose of hardship as a child or teenager helps build coping skills, resilience, and perspective to meet the challenge of dealing with debilitating, chronic pain in one's adult life.

Ice bucket test

Seery tested this hypothesis in another way. He asked respondents to hold their hands in a bucket of very cold water for five minutes. Those who reported a moderate number of negative life events showed less response to physical pain. Seery also had them take a high-stakes test in the lab. This same group was less likely to have a higher stress response when testing.

"Having faced moderate stress in the past seemed to help individuals cope with newly occurring stressors happening in the here and now," says Seery. "They seemed to have gained a sense that when bad things happen that doesn't mean it's always going to be that bad."

Justine was heartbroken when her alcoholic father left them when she was seven years old, and she hoped he would come back for years. It was a contentious divorce, and Justine's mother worried about Justine, so put them both in counseling soon into the divorce. While Justine resented this at first, she grew to like the "therapist lady" and after a while began to appreciate the lack of fighting in the house. In fact, when she would go to her dad's house on the weekend and listen to him fight with his new wife, she was glad to come home to her mom. When she was 14 years old, she decided not to keep going to her dad's every weekend because she found it too stressful and she wanted to spend more time with her friends. Her dad fought this, but her mom got them into mediation and a better visitation scheduled was worked out. As an adult working in addiction treatment, Justine knows it's important to stay connected with her Al-anon meetings and work with her sponsor if she is going to keep her "stuff" under control. Sometimes she feels the stress build up in her shoulders, so she goes and gets a massage and talks to her support system.

"We're not talking about the need to eliminate stress," he explains. "In children's lives, learning to deal with normative stress is part of healthy development." Normative stress helps kids learn to seek out resourceful strategies, self-soothe, recover and build the biological capacities for resilience. Toxic stress, however, occurs when a child's stress response systems are activated in the absence of supportive, calming relationships and stay activated for prolonged periods of time, and essentially becomes what life is usually like for a child. This is not the stress associated with a bad day. This is the stress associated with chronic activation of systems that disrupt brain circuits as they're developing and wears the body down.

Building Resilience

There are a variety of formal definitions of resilience, all of which focus on our capacity to bounce back from, or even grow, in the face of adverse circumstances. Rather than a set of characteristics, I would propose that resilience is a quality, and seeds are there even when we feel most broken or injured. This is a strengths-based perspective. I would acknowledge the scar tissue from trauma and early attachment disruptions, AND see the places where we continued to function well – even excel. Our potential resilience can be developed or impacted by: nature, the quality and amount of attachment relationships, the availability of other resources for interpersonal support, temperament, the capacity to regulate our emotions, and prior experience of trauma.

Because our potential to access our resilience is impacted by the internal and external resources we have available to us, we do not have to shift the stressors in life, which may not be possible, but we can increase our resources and even support or neurology to operate at our best in the face of the challenges in our life. We can create new neurons, make new synaptic connections, promote new patterns of thoughts and reactions, bring under-connected areas of the brain back online, and reset our stress response so that we decrease the inflammation that makes us ill.

We can develop our capacity for connection and attachment; we can address the physical trauma that continues to interrupt our immune system, and we can develop self-care strategies that increase the odds that we will thrive in our addiction counseling careers.

A place to Start: The Importance of Emotional Expression

Kennedy-Moore and Watson, emotional theorists, suggest that there are at least three ways in which emotional expression may ease our distress.

- It can reduce distress about distress (e.g. doing it and surviving it reduces fears about feeling in general).

- It can facilitate insight (e.g. vague feelings became clear, thus deepening self-knowledge and opening up possibilities for how to respond).

- It can enhance interpersonal relationships (e.g. though improved communication).

- Emotional expression also signifies to others one's state and associates need (e.g distress and the need for comfort or help or anger and need for a boundary) and releases resources, including adaptive strategies.

Felitti and Anda encourage a conversation between the health provider and the client to allow the emotional recognition of the impact of the ACE's in a client's life.

ACE Conversation

- How old was I at the time of these events?
- How likely is it that there are events I don't remember? (Implicit versus explicit memory)
- What was my relationship to the person or persons involved in the adversity I faced? Was someone you trusted and depended on for your survival a source of chronic, unpredictable stress?
- How much support did I receive from other caregivers in my life?

Just a conversation about the fact that ACEs matter in your current health can have enormous beneficial output. Asking, including asking about subjects we have been taught as children that nice people don't discuss, listening and accepting that person for who they are, in all their human complexity, are a powerful form of doing that confers great relief to patients. — Felitti

Mindfulness to Repair the Brain

Brain scans of individuals who faced childhood adversity often show a loss of interconnectivity in areas that are critical to creating loving relationships, activating a sense of calm in the face of stress and downshifting the inflammatory response. When these connections are underdeveloped we have little awareness of our own feelings and lack of consciousness about the effects of our behavior on others. We can't see how our defensive patterns of interacting are hurting those we care for and we can't see how they are hurting us — we lack insight into how we improve our relationships.

Mindfulness meditation helps us change our brain and bring the brain back online to reset our inflammation response.

Research shows that even though mindfulness practitioners still pumped out inflammatory hormones such as cortisol when stressed, their cortisol levels went down more quickly once the stressor had passed. Faster cortisol recovery means you can rebound more quickly from stressful situations. It means that you reduce the time that your body and mind are bathed in inflammatory chemicals, which leads to less physical and neural inflammation and less physical disease anxiety and depression.

When kids practice mindfulness they may strengthen the same circuits of the brain that were weakened by early adversity and childhood trauma — including the frontal lobe and the hippocampus.

You focus on your breath, note and name your thoughts, let them go, and see what remains when you are not thinking. You free yourself from worrying, spinning stories and ruminating. When you breathe deeply and bring oxygen into your lungs, that oxygen travels throughout the body, into the cells, where it supports all life-giving biological pathways. As you breathe in and out with long slow breaths through mindful breathing, you also strengthen and recharge the activity of your underactive para-sympathetic nervous system. We don't have a medicine that boosts the parasympathetic system (rest and recuperate) than this.

Mindsight™

According to Dan Siegel, those of us who have faced adversity develop what he calls Mindsight — the ability to truly see and know the mind. When you focus your attention on the mind and how it's working, it is possible to build specific circuits, repair neurocircuitry and grow connections among neurons in the same areas of the brain that tend to be weak due to early adversity, trauma, and insecure attachment.

The first aspect of Mindsight is insight, the ability to sense your own internal mental life and reflect inwardly — what you might think of as being self-aware or self-knowing.

The second is empathy, the ability to sense the inner mental life of another person, knowing who that person is.

The third is integration, the ability to link those two awarenesses and other processes into an interconnected picture.

Integration helps you approach problems reflectively and interact with others in wise, healthy ways. It promotes compassionate connections and communications. Integration helps you reconnect your past, present and future in coherent ways so that your life story makes sense of who you are. Siegel explains, "Mindsight enables us to go beyond "being sad" or "being angry" to recognize that we have these feelings of sadness or anger. Mindsight helps us see that they are not the totality of who we are, accept them for what they are and then allow them to transform so that do not lead to depression or rage."

When you are aware of what you feel when you are in tune with your inner world, you recognize when you're getting primed to react. You notice your heart rate is going up, your breathing is shallow, your muscles are tense, and so you pause, you take a deep breath, take a break and let yourself calm down.

"Tuning in to your own thoughts and those of others links different aspects of the brain and body that help with your capacity to be attuned to the world around you in a new way," says Siegel. "This allows for both personal well-being and healthier relationships."

Janet knows that she has a history of conflict with her coworkers though it is only recently that she has begun to think she might be part of the problem. She blamed the agency the last two times she was let go. In fact, she has been an "angry person" most of her life "for damn good reason" she would tell you. It's true, she had a hard upbringing with a lot of abuse and injustice. However, Janet's counselor is teaching her to see her anger as a defense — a strategy — and not a way of being. It is not her identity which gives Janet choices about her response in challenge situations. This knowledge opens up whole new opportunities for relationships with others, and Janet is curious to see if she can make this job last with the new skills she is learning.

When you examine feelings and thoughts, they are mental activities that create energy in the brain. "Ions flowing in and out of the membranes of our brain's basic cells, our neurons, leads to the release of chemicals that allow these neurons to communicate with one another," says Siegel. "That electrochemical energy helps to reconnect areas of the brain that are less connected due to early adversity, stimulating the growth of neurons and strengthening the brains."

Compassion Training

Compassion training requires you to work actively with your emotions and assumptions about yourself and others to release long-held resentments, hostility, and indifference. It helps you nurture compassion, understanding and a sense of connection with others, **and to develop a deep feeling of affection for yourself. It allows you, perhaps for the very first time in your life, to be on your side.**

Begin by focusing on the breath, hold an image of yourself in your mind and begin to wish yourself well, saying this set of phrases out loud:

- May I be filled with love and kindness
- May I be safe and protected

- May I love and be loved
- May I be happy and contented
- May I be healthy and strong
- May my life unfold with ease

Move your focus to someone you love dearly and hold that person in your mind's eye and repeat above.

Next bring to mind someone you don't know well, like the post officer or the person who cuts your hair and repeat above.

Now bring into your mind's eye someone with whom you have had relational trouble or discord, someone who has caused you pain, not trauma, and repeat above.

Extend your feelings of loving kindness to include all beings and repeat above.

Mending the Body Through the Gut

Recent science shows that a sophisticated neural network transmits messages from trillions of digestive bacteria to the brain, exerting a powerful influence on our state of mind and creating a feedback loop between the brain and the gut that goes both ways.

Emotional adversity, mental stress, and trauma lead to a greater proliferation of bad bacteria in the gut. Bad bugs in the gut lead to lower mood, anxiety, depression and a proclivity for being less resilient in the face of adversity and stress.

Why?

First, gut bacteria manufactures more than 80 percent of the body's supply of serotonin, which significantly influences mood. Second, good gut macrobiotics such as those found in probiotics, has a direct effect on neurotransmitter receptors in the brain such as GABA.

The messages between the gut and the brain are transmitted via the vagus nerve, which is a primary mediator of the inflammatory stress response.

That's why scientists have begun to refer to our gut as "the second brain." The gut microbiome heavily influences neural development, brain chemistry, emotional behavior, pain perception, learning and memory.

Improving our diet and reducing our intake of processed foods and sugar, and adding in greens, fruits and fermented food rich in probiotics, can play a critical role in healing the gut.

Because microorganisms in our gut control our brain, we need to do whatever we can to make our microbiome healthy and give the pathways in our brain all the serotonin and nutrients they need to send the correct messages along our brain's synapses.

Evelyn escaped her chaotic family by leaving for college at 18, and has been upwardly mobile since. She completed her studies and manages to work 50 hours week despite her IBS and chronically pot addicted and under functioning husband. While she is managing her IBS well, she is beginning to notice her resentment and loneliness in her marriage. She notices that her IBS flare-ups seem to be most severe and painful when she is paying bills and is aware of her husband's lack of participation. Evelyn begins to use her stomach symptoms as indicators that it is time to address her concerns and make some decisions about her life.

Connecting

When you begin to feel trust, perhaps for the first time in your life, and when this process is repeated, you modify old circuits in the brain that tell you that you cannot trust. You create new brain cells and connection that allow you to create new habits and responses to other people. Part of the power of therapy and a solid relationship is that one can learn, finally, as an adult to become attached to a safe person.

People can be part of the solution.

Martin has never thought getting a sponsor was necessary for him. He believes people need to work their program their way and doesn't want to give someone the power to "tell him what to do." However, he notices that his co-workers with more clean time and a sponsor seem to have better relationships than he does, and he is frustrated with another recent break-up. Maybe they know something he doesn't. So, he looks around at a meeting he attends and finds himself watching this older guy. This guy reminds him of his brother and wonders if that guy would be cool. He doesn't seem like a control freak, and he likes the way the guy talks about his wife, even when they're having problems. It's totally foreign to him. Martin gets up the nerve one night to ask the guy to be his "temporary" sponsor, giving himself a way out if it's too intense or the guy is psycho. The sponsor recognizes this in Martin and tells him that Martin will be in control of the relationship and how it develops. Martin can feel his gut begin to loosen up.

Somatic Experiencing™

Somatic experiencing allows us a safe way to discharge all the emotions and sensations we've stored during traumatic events so that we can begin to heal.

Clients are not asked to talk about their traumatic experience, but they learn about how their body regulates stress and to take note of the physical sensations, to tune into them and see what feelings, thoughts, and images arise. Slowly, and within an environment of safety, individuals learn to experience small amounts of that original distress and release that stored energy. Tolerating this distress allows their nervous system to return to balance. Over time, more and more of an individual's most difficult emotions begin to surface safely.

SOMATIC EXPERIENCING® (SE) psychobiological trauma resolution is a potent method for resolving trauma symptoms and relieving chronic stress. It is the life's work of Dr. Peter A. Levine, resulting from his multidisciplinary study of stress physiology, psychology, ethology, biology, neuroscience, indigenous healing practices and medical biophysics, *together with* more than 45 years of successful clinical application. The SE approach releases traumatic shock, which is key to transforming PTSD and the wounds of emotional and early developmental attachment trauma.

The SE Approach facilitates the completion of self-protective motor responses and the release of thwarted survival energy bound in the body, thus addressing the root cause of trauma symptoms. This is approached by gently guiding clients to develop increasing tolerance for difficult *bodily sensations and suppressed emotions.*

SE trauma resolution does not require the traumatized person to re-tell or re-live the traumatic event. Instead, it offers the opportunity to engage, complete and resolve, in a slow and supported way, the body's instinctual fight, flight and freeze responses. Individuals locked in anxiety or rage then relax into a growing sense of peace and safety.

Those stuck in depression gradually find their feelings of hopelessness and numbness transformed into empowerment, triumph, and mastery. SE trauma resolution catalyzes corrective bodily experiences that contradict those of fear and helplessness. This resolution resets the nervous system, restores inner balance, enhances resilience to stress and increases people's vitality, equanimity and capacity to actively engage in life.

Pendulation

In order to handle the physical sensations and memories that arise, individuals learn a process called "pendulation." With pendulation, they establish a "safe place" in their mind, a touch point that they can go to anytime to feel secure. This might be a memory of someone close to them or a benefactor who helped them, or a safe place they've been to or imagined or a place in nature. Alternatively, they might simply hold an object that helps to ground them in the present moment.

Clients pendulate back and forth between their safe place and the more difficult physical sensations and emotions that arise from past adversity and trauma. They learn to safely face and discharge that early stress so that their nervous system can return to a balanced state.

Somatic experiencing helps someone who has experienced trauma to slow down, experience painful sensations comfortably and to tolerate feelings without getting overwhelmed by them. When you feel safe enough to be aware of your feeling state, you can regulate your emotions and actions.

NeuroAffective Relational Model (NARM)R

NARM is a somatically based psychotherapy that focuses on supporting an individual's capacity for increasing connection and aliveness. To a degree, our five biologically-based core needs are met early in life and we develop core capacities that allow us to recognize and meet these needs as adults.

Connection, Attunement, Trust, Autonomy, Love-Sexuality

Being attuned to those five core basic needs and capacities means that we are connected to our deepest resources and vitality.

Five adaptive survival styles are set in motion depending on how well the five core basic need are met, or not met, in early life. The adaptive survival styles are ways of coping with the dysregulation, disconnection, disorganization and isolation a child experiences when these needs are not being met.

Core Needs – Caregiver Failure – Disconnection – Compromised Core Capacity – Adaptive Survival Style.

The NARM Model focuses on the interconnection of biological and psychological development. The NARM Model:

Clarifies the role of connections difficulties as they affect a person on all levels of experience: physiological, psychological and relational.

Develops the use of somatic mindfulness and orientation-forward personal strengths to increase the capacity for self-regulation and the freedom from the limitations of the fixed identities of adaptive learning styles.

Conclusion

I truly hope you have found this small book helpful as you take the time to take care of yourself. We need you and your gifts in the field. I would encourage you to create a small codependency treatment plan for yourself as you move forward, giving thought to what you most need to address to heal the internal system that drives your behavior. CHANGE IS POSSIBLE, even though codependency can feel cellular-level in depth. It will be a work in progress. You may need to enter Al-Anon and approach relationship work the same way you approached your addiction. Maybe you would be more comfortable in personal therapy or finding a professional codependency group.

Sample Codependency Treatment Plan

Developmentally:

Complete a family genogram and explore the attachment patterns, mental/substance abuse patterns and relationship patterns across at least three generations.

Explore ways in which I continue to "act out" those patterns in my current personal and professional life.

Behaviorally:

Complete the *Experiences in Close Relationships-Revised (ECR-R) Adult Attachment Questionnaire* found in Awakening Hope to identify my intimacy style.

Make a list of behaviors I recognize as I go through the symptoms, connecting them with my attachment style.

Work with someone to develop alternative strategies to correct these reactive behaviors.

Biologically:

Watch **Stress: Portrait of A Killer**
www.youtube.com/watch?v=eYG0ZuTv5rs

Get a physical exam, including blood work to identifying areas that need attention.

Create a physical movement plan to develop stamina and lower stress.

This book has been a summary of my approach to healing. If you want to read more about this, you could read:

Awakening Hope. A Developmental, Behavior, Biological Approach to Codependency Treatment, by Mary Crocker Cook

Codependency and Men, by Mary Crocker Cook

Resources

1. Heller, L. and LaPierre, A. Healing Developmental Trauma (2012) Berkeley, North Atlantic Books.

2. Mikulincer, M.; Shaver, P.R.; Pereg, D. (2003). "Attachment theory and affect regulation: The dynamics, development, and cognitive consequences of attachment-related strategies". Motivation and Emotion 27: 77–102.

3. Sapolsky, R.M. (2004) Why zebras don't get ulcers: An updated guide to stress. Stress related diseases and coping (3rd ed). New York, NY: Henry Holt & Co.

4. Felitti VJ, Anda RF, Nordenberg D, et al. Relationship of childhood abuse and household dysfunction to many of the leading causes of death in adults. The adverse childhood experiences (ACE) study. Am J Prev Med 1998;14:245--58.

5. Anda RF, Felitti VJ, Bremner JD, et al. The enduring effects of abuse and related experiences in childhood: a convergence of evidence from neurobiology and epidemiology. Eur Arch Psychiatry Clin Neurosci 2006;256:174--86.

6. Porges, S. (2001) The polyvagal theory: Phylogenetic substrates of a social nervous system. International Journal of Psychophysiology, 42, 123-146.

7. Cramer, S. C. , Sur, M. Dobkin, B.H., O'Brien, C. Spranger, T.D., et al. (2011) Harnessing neuroplasticity for clinical applications. Brain, 134 (6), 1591-1601.

8. M.D. Seery, R.J. Leo, S.P. Lupien, et.al, "An Upside to Adversity? Moderate Cumulative Lifetime Adversity Is Associated with Resilient Responses in the Face of Controlled Stressors," Psychological Science 24 mo. 7 (July 1, 2013), 1181-89.

9. Nakazawa, Donna J. Childhood Disrupted. (2015) New York, Atria Books

10. Reivich, K. and Shatte. A. (2003) The resilience factor: Seven keys to finding your inner strength and overcoming life's hurdles. New York, NY Broadway Books

11. Kennedy-Moore, E., & Warson, J.C. (2001) How and When does emotional expression help? Review of General Psychology, Vol. 5, No. 3, 187-212.

12. Seigel, Danial. J. *The Developing Mind: Toward a Neurobiology of Interpersonal Experience* (1999) New York: Guilford Press

13. Schore, Allan. Affect Dysregulation and Disorders of the Self. (2003) W.W. Norton

14. Heinrich, M. , von Dawans, B., & Domes, G. (2009). Oxytocin, vasopressin, and human social behavior. Frontiers in Neuroendocrinology, 30 (4), 548-557.

15. Lee, H.J., Macbeth, A.H., Pagini, J.H., & Young, W.S. (2009) Oxytocin: the great facilitator of life. Progress in Neurobiology, 88 (2), 127-151.

16. Seigel, Danial. J. *The Developing Mind: Toward a Neurobiology of Interpersonal Experience* (1999) New York: Guilford Press

17. Banenoch, Bonnie. Being a Brain-Wise Therapist: A Practical Guide to Interpersonal Neurobiology(2008) Norton Series on Interpersonal Neurobiology.

18. Bradshaw, John. Bradshaw On: The Family: A New Way of Creating Solid Self-Esteem (1990). HCI.

19. Ruth Buczynski, PhD and Ruth Lanius, MD, Ph.D. http://nicabm-stealthseminar.s3.amazonaws.com/Trauma2012/Lanius/NICABM-Lanius2012.pdf

20. Cozolino, Louis J. The Neuroscience of Human Relationships: Attachment and the Developing Social Brain (2006)WW Norton, pg. 235

21. *Flores, P. J. (2001). Addiction as an attachment disorder: Implications for group therapy. International Journal of Group Psychotherapy, 51(1), pg. 70.*

22. What is Mindsight? An Interview with Dan Siegel. http://www.psychalive.org/what-is-mindsight-an-interview-with-dr-dan-siegel/

23. Somatic Experiencing Trauma Institute. http://traumahealing.org/

24. http://insightcenter.org/NARM/

About the Author

If you wish to contact Mary please feel free to call, send an email, or write to:

Mary Crocker Cook
1710 Hamilton Ave. #8
San Jose, CA 95125.

Phone: (408) 448-0333

Email:
marycook@connectionscounselingassociates.com

For more information about Mary's counseling services or presentation topics visit:

www.marycrockercook.com

CPSIA information can be obtained
at www.ICGtesting.com
Printed in the USA
FSOW01n0035310316
18571FS

9 781611 702255